T0041884

THE KETO CARNIVORE COOKBOOK

KETO CARNIVORE COOKBOOK

Low-Carb Recipes, Tips, and a 6-Week Meal Plan to Boost Your Diet Success

MEL BROWN

PHOTOGRAPHY BY MARIJA VIDAL

ROCKRIDGE PRESS

Copyright © 2021 by Rockridge Press, Emeryville, California

No part of this publication may be reproduced, stored in a retrieval system, or transmitted in any form or by any means, electronic, mechanical, photocopying, recording, scanning, or otherwise, except as permitted under Sections 107 or 108 of the 1976 United States Copyright Act, without the prior written permission of the Publisher. Requests to the Publisher for permission should be addressed to the Permissions Department, Rockridge Press, 6005 Shellmound Street, Suite 175, Emeryville, CA 94608.

Limit of Liability/Disclaimer of Warranty: The Publisher and the author make no representations or warranties with respect to the accuracy or completeness of the contents of this work and specifically disclaim all warranties, including without limitation warranties of fitness for a particular purpose. No warranty may be created or extended by sales or promotional materials. The advice and strategies contained herein may not be suitable for every situation. This work is sold with the understanding that the Publisher is not engaged in rendering medical, legal, or other professional advice or services. If professional assistance is required, the services of a competent professional person should be sought. Neither the Publisher nor the author shall be liable for damages arising herefrom. The fact that an individual, organization, or website is referred to in this work as a citation and/or potential source of further information does not mean that the author or the Publisher endorses the information the individual, organization, or website may provide or recommendations they/it may make. Further, readers should be aware that websites listed in this work may have changed or disappeared between when this work was written and when it is read.

For general information on our other products and services or to obtain technical support, please contact our Customer Care Department within the United States at (866) 744-2665, or outside the United States at (510) 253-0500.

Rockridge Press publishes its books in a variety of electronic and print formats. Some content that appears in print may not be available in electronic books, and vice versa.

TRADEMARKS: Rockridge Press and the Rockridge Press logo are trademarks or registered trademarks of Callisto Media Inc. and/or its affiliates, in the United States and other countries, and may not be used without written permission. All other trademarks are the property of their respective owners. Rockridge Press is not associated with any product or vendor mentioned in this book.

Interior and Cover Designer: Lindsey Dekker
Art Producer: Sara Feinstein
Editor: Justin Hartung
Production Editor: Emily Sheehan
Production Manager: Jose Olivera

Photography © 2021 Marija Vidal. Food styling by Victoria Woollard
Title Page: Photography by Marija Vidal

ISBN: Print 978-1-64876-409-7 | eBook 978-1-64876-410-3
R1

To my family, who remained brutally honest
when it came to testing out recipes.
Thank you for your love, support, and
patience during this process.
You now have your Mama back.

CONTENTS

INTRODUCTION

Welcome to the world of health and nutrition. Simply acknowledging that you want to make a change in your lifestyle is a great first step. Before you start researching on the internet, which is full of conflicting information, you first need to figure out your "why." Do you want to feel healthy and strong? Do you want to lose weight? Do you struggle with sleep problems, anxiety, or depression? Are you an athlete and want to improve your performance? Whatever your reason for exploring a healthier way to eat, I applaud you for taking the first step.

I am a woman in my 40s, with five children and a new granddaughter. I mention my age because I want people to know that making positive changes in your life can happen at any point in your life journey. I yo-yo dieted my entire adult life. Nothing would stick for me. I would always end up putting the weight back on that I had lost. I was consistently tired. By 4 p.m. each day my energy levels were low. I have always exercised moderately, and because I have such a large family, I was always active. Yet I did not feel like my best self. I struggled a little with anxiety, and my relationship with food was poor. I used food as a crutch to make myself feel better in times of sadness, when I was tired, or simply when I was bored.

As a result, I decided to research the ketogenic diet. I gathered information and began my journey four years ago. Today, I am the healthiest I have ever been, in body and in mind. My relationship with food is a positive one. I enjoy eating food, I enjoy talking about food, and I enjoy cooking food. I no longer use food as a crutch to feed negative emotions. And I now support thousands of people on their own journeys to improve their overall health and relationship with food.

I have always enjoyed creating recipes and now I particularly enjoy converting my most-loved recipes into keto recipes. To me, food is love. Food is a celebration of families coming together and creating memories. The meals that you share with your family and friends can shape the most significant moments in your life. Food is also fuel and energy for your body. The foods you eat dictate how you feel physically, mentally, and emotionally. And only you can determine what those foods are. Learning to fuel myself with good fats and proteins—rather than depleting myself of necessary calories—was life changing.

Once I had lived the ketogenic lifestyle for a couple of years, I realized that it was truly possible to improve the way I ate. I wanted to interrupt the cycle of eating too many desserts, and reduce the amount of artificial sweeteners in my diet. It was causing bloat and stalling my weight loss journey. So, I refined my keto diet, began

a keto carnivore lifestyle, and stuck to eating whole foods and cleaner ingredients. I noticed a significant improvement in my focus, sleep quality, and energy levels, and it broke through my weight loss plateau, too.

This book will help you on your own journey to discover which foods work well for you and which cause negative reactions in your body. You'll do this by resetting the way you eat, first by eliminating foods and then by reintroducing them to see how each makes you feel. This book's 6-week reset plan will serve as a road map for your journey, taking you from super-simple carnivore eating to a clean keto diet. And while I've provided recipe suggestions for those 6 weeks, you can customize the plan to your specific tastes and preferences using the book's 75 recipes.

It's important to note: The carnivore diet is not the best choice for everyone. Those in the middle of pregnancy or who need to limit their protein intake should avoid it, to name a few. I advise you to always consult a doctor before starting any kind of restrictive diet.

I wish you well on this exciting journey. Please connect with me on Instagram (@ladymelskitchen) and reach out if you have any questions.

PART 1

The Keto Carnivore Way

In this section I will explain why keto and carnivore work so well together. Carnivore is often seen as a natural progression from keto. I will also provide a 6-week reset plan to guide you through the beginning of your own journey.

Clockwise from left: Sizzling Salmon, page 93; Whole Roast Chicken, page 76; Dill Dip, page 115

CHAPTER 1

Connecting Keto and Carnivore

In this chapter we will explore both the keto and carnivore diets. We will look at the similarities between the two, showing how the carnivore diet can be specifically used as a reset diet. A reset diet is used to highlight food intolerances, kick-start your metabolism, target weight loss, or address medical problems you may be experiencing. By eliminating foods and then reintroducing them, you can identify foods that have become problematic for you. If you are happy with your health and simply wish to dive straight into lots of highly nutritious and delicious keto and carnivore recipes, jump to part 2 (page 37) and start cooking!

The 21st-Century Carnivore

There are many possible reasons you may have been drawn to this book. You may have been on keto for a while now and are starting to notice your progress slowing down. Maybe you are having difficulty with discipline and portion control, or you still have a sweet tooth and consume too many keto treats. Or you may be looking for a way to identify problematic ingredients you are eating on your current keto plan. Perhaps you are an athlete looking to improve your performance, recovery, and healing.

You may have heard about the carnivore diet and wondered what it entails. While it may seem unrealistic or overly limited at first, my aim throughout this book is to show you how the carnivore diet works when combined with keto and I'll highlight the many benefits you will see as a result. It can enhance your weight loss or help you break through a plateau. It can also improve your concentration and clarity and even promote better quality of sleep.

When used as a reset diet, the carnivore diet can help you address food intolerances and digestive issues as well as improve your overall health. Gradually, you'll begin to introduce more foods and note how they make you feel. The ultimate goal is to identify a reset plan that works well for your body and is sustainable long term. Whether you choose to continue eating on the carnivore diet or move to clean keto, I will offer tips for creating a sustainable eating plan.

You may doubt your discipline and you may even doubt that this way of eating can work. You may think that it's too limiting. But I know you can do it and I know it works because it worked for me. You will feel great eating carnivore and you will definitely be enjoying your food along the way.

Keto and Carnivore, Side by Side

This section will cover the similarities and differences between the keto and carnivore diets. I will explain the guidelines for each diet, and highlight the potential benefits of both. I have personally done both keto and carnivore diets, and while I mostly eat clean keto, I dip in and out of doing the carnivore diet when I need something stricter for a period of time. Both the keto and carnivore diets restrict carbs and encourage high-fat, high-protein intake. This combination, along with the absence of grains, processed foods, and sugars, creates a metabolic shift in your body: one that changes how you burn energy.

A BRIEF HISTORY

While human evolution has had carnivorous eating at its core for over two and a half million years, the carnivore diet wasn't offered as an eating plan until 1856. Bernard Moncriff, a German author, published a book in London called *The Philosophy of the Stomach*. He believed that eating a diet consisting of only meat, fish, and other animal products cured him of his ailments. The carnivore diet stems from the belief that we are at our healthiest when we eat animal products only.

The carnivore diet differs from other low-carb diets in that it aims for a zero-carb intake. Other low-carb diets (including keto) allow for some carbs, whereas the carnivore diet restricts them totally. Followers of a strict carnivore diet believe that by eating only animal products, the body is getting everything it requires. With the high intake of protein, you will feel fuller longer, and therefore you'll consume fewer overall calories. This, in turn, can lead to increased metabolism and weight loss.

More recently, the carnivore diet gained new popularity after Joe Rogan hosted a 2018 podcast with Dr. Shawn Baker, an elite athlete, medical doctor, and author of the best-selling book *The Carnivore Diet*. Now, more and more people are enjoying the benefits of a carnivore lifestyle.

A KETO RECAP

While you may be familiar with the keto diet, it's worth revisiting the basics before you learn how it can be combined with the carnivore diet. The ketogenic diet significantly reduces carbs from your diet. This forces your body to burn fat instead of glucose for energy. This is called being in *ketosis* and becoming *fat adapted*. Historically the diet was designed to treat epilepsy, but it has also been known to treat autism, migraines, brain trauma, and stroke. More commonly, it's used to assist with weight loss, sleep problems, anxiety, inflammation, and mental clarity, so you can see there are many benefits when you adopt this way of eating.

There are different approaches to the diet, ranging from *relaxed* to *clean keto*. It depends on the amount of carbs you allow yourself and the limitations on ingredients. For example, I tend to follow clean keto. This means that I do not eat wheat, grains, or any processed foods. The few carbs I do eat are in the form of berries and green vegetables. Someone who eats a more relaxed version of keto may permit wheat and grains in their diet and they enjoy desserts that use certain sweeteners to replace sugar, as well as nut flours to replace processed flour. Relaxed ketoers also tend to consume a higher carb count per day.

This brings us to a discussion on macros, your rough guide to how many macronutrients you should consume. Broadly speaking, in a keto diet, 65 percent of your calories should come from fat, 30 percent from protein, and 5 percent from carbs. These percentages can be altered to suit your needs, but in general, the fewer carbs you eat, the better the diet works. Some people do well with more protein, and I urge you to listen to your body in this matter. We all metabolize foods differently. These macros are a platform for you to begin your journey. From there, you can adapt the percentages to find the right balance for you.

INTRODUCING CARNIVORE

The carnivore diet is a more restrictive eating plan than keto. It limits ingredients to meat, fish, and other animal products, such as eggs, some cheeses, limited amounts of heavy cream, and some dry seasonings. It excludes all fruits, vegetables, grains, nuts, and seeds. It is practically a zero-carb diet, and therefore can offer faster results than keto. Some people like to be extremely strict on the carnivore diet by eating only meat, salt, and water. More commonly, though, all animal products can be eaten and enjoyed.

A few benefits of the carnivore diet that don't apply to the keto diet include the high absorption of nutrients in our foods, better sleep, more focus and mental clarity, and the simplicity of the diet. Macros don't need to be tracked when eating this way, which is definitely a plus in my book. You will also notice a decrease in appetite, largely due to the amount of meat you're consuming. The protein and fat from animal products keep you fuller for a longer period of time, so you will find that your desire to snack in between meals will vanish. As you begin to eat less, your overall calorie intake will decrease. I personally find that the carnivore diet is the only eating plan I have followed in which I was not hungry between meals. The food I eat now is the perfect amount that my body requires, due to the fact that animal products are nutritionally dense.

By cutting out glucose, seed oils, and processed foods, you will support your health and wellness journey. You may see improved focus and clarity, a boost in your energy levels, and improved sleep. That, along with all the anti-inflammatory benefits this diet can bring, makes weight loss seem like an added bonus.

The most important foundation of the carnivore diet is the pure nutritional value in the foods you will eat. Nutritional value is related to the quality of food you eat and the amount of nutrition your body receives. For example, liver is one of the most nutrient-dense foods you can eat. (See a wonderful Chicken Liver Pâté on page 75.) Plus it has high bioavailability, which means its nutrients are efficiently absorbed into your body. The bioavailability of key nutrients is significantly higher for humans when they eat animal products than when they eat plants. Your ability to absorb nutrients from a steak with 20 grams of protein is highly superior to a processed, packaged product that shows 20 grams of protein on the label.

This diagram shows where these diets overlap and where they differ:

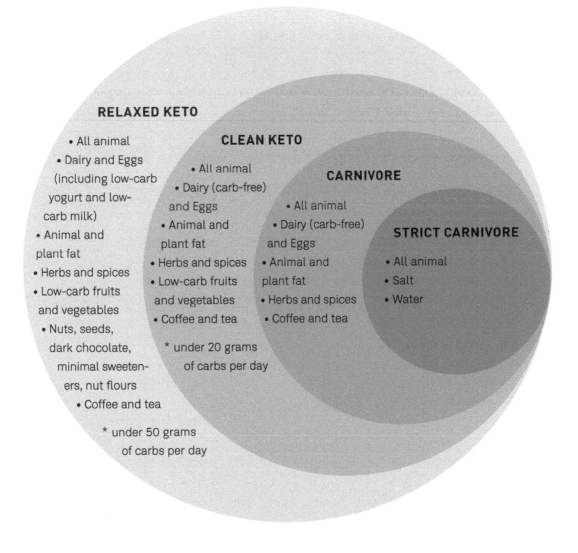

RELAXED KETO

- All animal
- Dairy and Eggs (including low-carb yogurt and low-carb milk)
- Animal and plant fat
- Herbs and spices
- Low-carb fruits and vegetables
- Nuts, seeds, dark chocolate, minimal sweeteners, nut flours
- Coffee and tea

* under 50 grams of carbs per day

CLEAN KETO

- All animal
- Dairy (carb-free) and Eggs
- Animal and plant fat
- Herbs and spices
- Low-carb fruits and vegetables
- Coffee and tea

* under 20 grams of carbs per day

CARNIVORE

- All animal
- Dairy (carb-free) and Eggs
- Animal and plant fat
- Herbs and spices
- Coffee and tea

STRICT CARNIVORE

- All animal
- Salt
- Water

The Carnivore Reset

I recommend approaching the carnivore diet as a stepping-stone to reaching an end goal. There are a multitude of reasons that someone might want to temporarily eat a diet almost entirely of animal products, including weight loss plateaus, digestive issues, GERD or reflux, autoimmune disorders, low energy levels, poor sleep patterns, and emotional or mental health challenges. This book uses a 6-week carnivore reset plan to walk you through the process.

Shifting from keto to carnivore means eliminating certain foods that you normally eat, and then slowly reintroducing them. The inclusion of certain foods may sit well for one person yet have surprising and significant negative effects for another. To get to the bottom of which foods may be the issue, one has to start at the beginning, and eat only the core basics of meat, salt, and water. Once your health issues improve, other foods or food subgroups can be slowly reintroduced, step by step. If the improvements continue when these items are brought back in, you'll know which foods work long term for you. Week by week, you'll test additional foods, seeing what works best for you and your needs.

Here are a few reasons to try the carnivore diet as a reset:

- **Lose Weight.** Weight loss can accelerate on the carnivore diet, simply because your body works more efficiently when it's fed only its most basic and pure nutritional needs, which are animal products. Quite rapidly, your hunger drops, resulting in your consuming less food.

- **Relieve Health Issues.** Many autoimmune and inflammatory issues are caused by foods other than animal products. The carnivore diet simply eliminates them all and resets your system. When you eliminate inflammatory ingredients such as sugar, grains, seed oils, and nightshades, your system will begin to reset.

- **Easy to Start.** One of the greatest things about the carnivore diet is its simplicity. Many followers actually enjoy the reduced number of meals, fewer choices, and straightforward foods. It means less to plan and think about in the kitchen.

STAGE-BY-STAGE EATING PLAN

The reset plan in chapter 2 will help you navigate the week-by-week process, offering simple and delicious recipes along the way. Weeks 1 to 4 offer varying degrees of all-meat eating; weeks 5 and 6 reintroduce some foods and follow the keto diet. Weeks 5 and 6 also give you an idea of how to continue eating after the plan finishes, so you can focus on a clean keto diet.

Here is an overview of the plan:

Week 1: Beef and other ruminants only. This week you will not only eliminate the greatest amount of food, you will also put your body into a state of detox.

Week 2: All meats. This week you will reintroduce different proteins, such as chicken and fish. Note how you feel after each meal.

Week 3: All meat, eggs, and low-sugar dairy products (such as butter or sour cream). This is an important week because your body will tell you what, if any, problems it has with dairy. Dairy is a common food intolerance and one to look out for.

Week 4: All meat, eggs, and low-sugar dairy products, low-sugar spices, and condiments. This week sets you up for a broader spectrum of foods before you go into the longer-term stages of clean keto.

Weeks 5 and 6: Traditional clean keto. These two weeks will include some fruit and vegetables as part of your daily diet.

Low-Carb in the Long Run

When it comes to eating low-carb as a permanent lifestyle, there are some specific things to consider, based on your experiences and goals. I recommend you work your way through the reset plan in chapter 2. If you are already a low-carb eater, begin at week 1 as suggested. The fact that you are already restricting carbs will help you navigate through week 1 without an intense detox.

If you currently eat a version of what is commonly known as the standard American diet, I recommend starting at week 2, and then doing two weeks of week 3. It is important that you track your symptoms along the way (see Tracking Your Symptoms, page 11). Make note of how you feel after you've introduced each new food. Once you've reached week 6 on the reset plan, you will be ready to think about what comes next. Clean keto or carnivore?

CHOOSING CLEAN KETO

Following a version of clean keto works well in many ways. It includes a wide variety of foods that allows the diet to become a sustainable lifestyle. Your nutritional needs will be met, and now that you have worked out which foods don't agree with you, you can simply avoid them. Clean keto avoids all seed oils and processed foods, and encourages you to buy good-quality food without pesticides and herbicides. Traditional keto simply limits carbs, perhaps without the restriction of grains, certain oils, and toxins. Clean keto focuses on the quality of food as well as on restricting the carb count.

GOING STRICT CARNIVORE

Perhaps you really enjoyed eating strict carnivore more than you thought you would. The human body is intuitive, and it may be that you are living your best life as a carnivore eater. Go with it! Use the reset plan for weeks 1 to 4 to create a version that best suits your lifestyle.

TRACKING YOUR SYMPTOMS

Now that you are in the habit of tracking your symptoms, be mindful to continue with this practice after the 6-week reset. You may find that eating too much dairy doesn't agree with you, but small amounts are okay. You may feel more energized when you eat lots of red meat rather than fish. I suggest that you record this information. You can simply make notes on your phone or make a spreadsheet with all the basic foods you eat and see if a specific food causes you a recurring problem. If it does, don't eat it as often, and see if that helps. If that doesn't resolve the problem, then cut out that food completely for one week. If the symptom you were experiencing goes away, then you'll know to avoid that particular food, at least for now. You can actually try reintroducing those foods at a future date and repeat the process to see if anything has changed.

When tracking your symptoms, look out for foods that seem to be inflammatory for you. Dairy is a common one. It could be a food group that you need to limit rather than eliminate completely. If I notice a particular food is causing me a problem, I reduce it for one week and pay attention to how bloated I feel at the end of each day. If I feel good, then I will continue to eat that food only in limited quantities and otherwise continue to eat as usual the following week.

This is how the carnivore reset can work for you as a tool moving forward. By tracking your symptoms, you'll have the knowledge and skills to recognize when your diet is causing you a problem. As time goes on, you may decide to revisit the 6-week reset plan. Perhaps you have allowed too many extra foods to creep back into your diet, or maybe your discipline with the quantity or quality of food has slipped. Whatever your reason, the plan is there when you need it.

FAQ: Macros, Supplements, and Intermittent Fasting

Here are answers to some common questions around nutrition, lifestyle habits, and most importantly, coffee! Since I am an avid coffee drinker, I'm going to address that topic first. Notice that the answers to these questions may differ, depending on whether you are eating carnivore or clean keto.

Q: Can I drink coffee, tea, or alcohol?

A: The simple answer regarding coffee across the board is yes. Whether you are keto or carnivore, even during intermittent fasting, black coffee is on the table. Black tea is also allowed. While eating carnivore, I would not recommend alcohol. During more relaxed stages of keto, small amounts of liquor (zero-sugar), dry wines, or dry champagnes are allowed.

Q: Should I be doing intermittent fasting?

A: If you have been doing keto for a while, and you use this book to work through the carnivore diet, I recommend intermittent fasting. If you begin this book as a newcomer to the low-carb life, let yourself be led by how you feel—many people discover that the desire to drop a meal (usually breakfast) kicks in very quickly. Benefits of intermittent fasting include faster weight loss, improved sleep, decreased appetite, improved concentration, lower levels of insulin, and increased cell repair, just to name a few. Eating carnivore is so satiating that the majority of people fall into intermittent fasting naturally. For this reason, I have included two meals a day within the first four weeks of the reset. You might continue with that as you journey back into keto.

Q: Do I need to track macros during the reset plan?

A: You do not. One of the plus sides of the carnivore diet is that you do not need to track macros. It's almost impossible to eat too much when you eat high amounts of animal products because you feel full quicker and for longer. When you enter weeks 5 and 6, you will need to start tracking your food. That could be full macros or just a carb count. Do what works for you. There are some great apps for this to keep it simple. Carb Manager is a good app to check out.

Q: Do I need to take any supplements?

A: I would recommend taking electrolytes. Assuming you manage to get outside in the sun daily to get the benefits of vitamin D, the foods that you are now eating should provide the necessary vitamins and minerals you need. Electrolytes are mainly made up of sodium, potassium, and magnesium. When you enter into ketosis on the keto diet, you will excrete carbs through your urine, sweat, and breath. When you expel ketones in your breath, it is commonly known as "keto breath." Your breath will smell like acetone and it is a sign of high levels of ketones in your blood. This symptom does pass. Although you will lose a lot of water and feel less bloated, you are also losing necessary electrolytes. It is important to replenish them. Use a pure and high-quality electrolyte supplement. Without this you will start to feel the symptoms of "keto flu."

Q: What is keto flu?

A: Keto flu is a common symptom for those on a restrictive carb diet, especially in the early phases or after a significant change in macros. The symptoms can include minor headaches, fatigue, and dizziness. To combat keto flu, be sure to drink plenty of water and take electrolyte supplements.

Q: What types of oil should I be using?

A: Seed oils, also known as vegetable oils or nut oils, are damaging to human health. They raise our omega-6 fatty acids to dangerous levels, which can cause issues in a multitude of ways. Some of the most common oils are soybean, canola, peanut, sunflower, and sesame. The only oils that should be consumed on this diet are from fruits (olive oil, coconut oil, avocado oil), or animals (butter, lard, tallow, and so forth).

Q: Do I need to exercise?

A: For optimal health during the plan (and always, really), I recommend getting 30 minutes of exercise a day. If you are a beginner to fitness, simply make it a goal to get moving each day. Exercise is a very personal thing. Choose types you enjoy and vary them in your schedule. Some examples are using home weights, joining cardio classes, or taking the dog for a walk. If you are an athlete or go to the gym regularly, you will enjoy an improvement in your ability and performance on the carnivore or keto diet.

Q: Will a carnivore diet help with a leaky gut?

A: Many people have reported that a low-carb lifestyle has helped alleviate symptoms of leaky gut. The reason for this is that when you consume a low-carb diet, you reduce the amount of toxins and increase your intake of anti-inflammatory foods. You are also eating healthier fats. This can all contribute to helping with leaky gut.

Q: How will this lifestyle impact my heart health?

A: When you eat a keto carnivore diet, there is significant evidence that your HDL levels (commonly known as good cholesterol) increase and your triglycerides (universally used as a negative health marker) decrease. According to *The Great Cholesterol Con* by Malcolm Kendrick, this improved ratio is a significant indication of improved cardiovascular health. But it's important to note that you should always consult expert medical advice if you have existing health issues and want to make changes in your diet.

KNOW YOUR TERMS: RUMINANTS AND OFFAL

Ruminants are cloven-hooved, four-legged animals that eat grass. They include cattle, sheep, and goats, and each has a unique digestive system that allows them to gain optimum energy from their food source.

Nutrient-rich meats from ruminants are popular in carnivore diets, because they provide a near-perfect balance of all the macronutrients and micronutrients a human requires. Macronutrients are the basic proteins and fats in your diet. Micronutrients, of which there are hundreds, include things like B vitamins, cholesterol, iron, zinc, vitamin D, omega-3s, magnesium, and potassium. These essential nutrients are highly bioavailable from ruminants.

Offal is organ meat. Believe it or not, it can be delicious. There are different types of organ meat, including liver, heart, kidneys, brain, and tongue, to name a few. Their strong flavors are not for everyone, but offal is nutrient-dense with very high bioavailability of vitamins B_{12}, A, D, E, and K; these are fat-soluble, which means your body can readily absorb them.

Liver is the most nutrient-dense organ meat, and it's a great source of vitamin A. It contains folic acid, iron, copper, zinc, and more. Rich in B vitamins, heart has been found to reduce the risk of Alzheimer's, dementia, anxiety, and depression. Kidneys provide plenty of omega-3 fatty acids and contain anti-inflammatory properties. Finally, brain and tongue are both rich in vitamins and minerals.

Talk to your local butcher and ask them to save you the offal meats you want. They often get discarded, so you should be able to buy them at a good price. Your butcher may even have some cooking tips. I have included a couple of simple and delicious offal recipes in this book for you to enjoy.

About the Recipes

Part 2 of this book offers a comprehensive collection of recipes for you to follow. I have been mindful to choose ingredients that are readily available. Many of the recipes are firm favorites in my house, and I cook them regularly for my family. A mixture of carnivore and clean keto recipes; they are simple and easy to follow. You can choose some of your favorite recipes and eat them repeatedly, or simply work your way through all the recipes.

The clean keto recipes can be enjoyed at the end of the reset plan, during weeks 5 and 6. They will provide the basis for your food plan as you move forward. You can eventually use the recipes to create your own long-term meal plan.

Each recipe is clearly labeled to indicate which phases of the carnivore reset plan it is suitable for. The chapters are organized to start with recipes that can be used at the beginning of the plan. The labels listed here indicate that a recipe includes certain ingredients or follows clean keto:

C1: beef and other ruminants, plus salt

C2: all meats, poultry, seafood, and salt

C3: all meats, poultry, seafood, salt, eggs, and low-sugar dairy products

C4: all meats, poultry, seafood, salt, eggs, and low-sugar dairy products, spices, and condiments

CK: follows the guidelines of a clean keto diet

Note: For some of the C1 and C2 recipes, I have provided options to add herbs and spices once you have moved past the initial strict reset phase. It won't change the nutritional value of the meal or affect your macros. It will just enhance and upgrade the flavors in the dish.

CHAPTER 2

6-Week Reset Plan

In this chapter, you will learn how to use a 6-week reset plan as an elimination diet to see if you have reactions to certain foods. This diet will also restart your weight loss if you've plateaued. It begins with strict carnivore eating, moves on to a less restrictive carnivore phase, and concludes with clean keto eating, which may be the way you choose to eat all the time as you move forward.

About the Plan

The reset plan is devised for one person, with enough for leftovers. Each week includes recipe suggestions for every meal, plus a shopping list. I've included only two meals per day. This is because you'll be less hungry while eating carnivore, and if you're doing intermittent fasting (see pages 12 and 19), which many keto dieters practice, you'll already be used to eating twice a day. That said, I recommend you eat when you are hungry and use the planner as a guide and not necessarily an absolute. Add a meal if you feel that your body needs it.

During weeks 1 and 2—the most restrictive part of the plan—you will be eating meat only. The plan begins with red meats for one week and then adds poultry and fish in the second week. You should take notes on how you feel, physically and mentally, after each introduction, which will help you get a sense of which animal products work well for you and which might be problematic. Bear in mind that at this point of the reset you will be detoxing and could be experiencing symptoms related to that rather than to actual food intolerances.

With the introduction of eggs, some cheese, heavy cream, and spices, weeks 3 and 4 are my favorites. You will enjoy a wide range of foods and meals without feeling restricted. This is how I eat most of the time now.

During weeks 5 and 6—the clean keto weeks—you will really enjoy reintroducing foods that have been eliminated. As you add back each food, note how you are feeling. This clean keto approach represents how you may want to eat all the time as you move forward. (See Low-Carb in the Long Run, page 9.)

Finally, remember that the recipes in the reset plan are merely suggestions. You can switch out any recipe that has the correct designation, as indicated by the recipe labels C1, C2, C3, C4, and CK.

Managing Expectations

The end results of this plan, that is, identifying any problematic foods and restarting weight loss, make the reset worthwhile. You may be nervous about side effects, but they should be mild. Most detox and elimination diets can cause headaches, lethargy, frustration, hunger (or alternately, lack of hunger), tiredness, or brain fog. You may experience some of these symptoms in the first few days of the reset. However, do your best to be relaxed about how you are feeling, knowing that any side effects will pass, and keep powering through. Try to avoid activities that require extra concentration in those first couple of days. You will quickly drop water weight, so replenishing fluids and minerals in the form of an electrolyte supplement needs to be a priority and will help minimize your symptoms. Before you know it, you'll be through the detox stage and begin to reap the rewards.

As you progress through the reset plan, you'll notice that your appetite will begin to shrink. When that happens, eat when you are hungry. Intuitive eating becomes second nature as you progress through the weeks. Eat when you are hungry and stop when you are full. Be in sync with your body and try to remain open to a new eating schedule. Most people are satisfied with two meals a day during carnivore. Eating those meals within an eight-hour window is called intermittent fasting. By eating within a shorter window of time, you allow your body to renew immune system cells and use fat for fuel. This, in turn, can accelerate weight loss, improve mental clarity and focus, help you sleep better, and increase your energy levels.

I am a firm believer in tracking success in ways other than the scales. For weight loss I recommend taking before and after pictures. Another way to track your progress is by taking a few body measurements, including the circumferences of your waist, arms, legs, and hips. Compare these measurements from the last day of your reset to those from your first day.

Lastly, success is not measured only by weight loss. Be proud of your journey, your positive mindset, and your commitment to this lifestyle. And keep in mind that there are many health benefits that may not be immediately apparent, including the fact that you are improving the chances that you will stay healthy longer as you age.

Week 1: Beef and Other Ruminants, Salt (C1)

This is an important week as you begin your journey. Listen to your body in terms of hunger, proper rest, and the crucial need to hydrate and get enough electrolytes. Most recipes yield two servings, which helps with meal prep, as you will have leftovers for another meal. Alternatively, you can always halve the recipe to yield one serving instead of two, if you prefer.

WEEK 1	MEAL 1	MEAL 2
MONDAY	Perfect Ground Beef (page 109)	Strip Steak (page 55), 1 serving
TUESDAY	Roasted Bone Marrow (page 57) with *Perfect Ground Beef leftovers*	The Naked Burger (page 58), 1 serving
WEDNESDAY	Perfect Ground Beef (page 109)	Bone-In Rib Eye (page 56)
THURSDAY	*Bone-In Rib Eye leftovers*	*Perfect Ground Beef leftovers*
FRIDAY	Delicious Sirloin (page 54)	Leg of Lamb (page 71)
SATURDAY	Roasted Bone Marrow (page 57) with *Leg of Lamb leftovers*	*Delicious Sirloin leftovers*
SUNDAY	Strip Steak (page 55), 1 serving, with *Roasted Bone Marrow leftovers*	The Naked Burger (page 58), 1 serving

SHOPPING LIST

MEAT

- Bone-in rib eye,
  2 (1-pound) steaks
- Ground 80/20 chuck
  beef (3 pounds)

- Lamb leg steak,
  2 (1-pound) steaks
- Marrow bones
  (4 pounds)

- Sirloin steaks,
  2 (10-ounce) steaks
- Strip steaks,
  2 (8-ounce) steaks

PANTRY

- Kosher salt

WHAT TO KNOW

Digestion: You may experience constipation or diarrhea during this first week. To help with the adjustment, make sure that you are drinking plenty of water and taking your electrolytes.

Appetite: This first week you may find yourself thinking of nothing but food. If you are hungry, definitely eat. Try to eat two larger meals rather than snacking on small meals. Eat as much as you need to be full.

Electrolytes: You must take electrolytes daily. Because insulin levels are lower in a carnivore diet, our kidneys excrete critical electrolytes in the form of sodium, potassium, and magnesium.

Hydration: Always stay well hydrated. During week 1, you may feel thirsty as your kidneys expel excess water as your insulin levels come down. Water will help combat headaches, transport nutrients, and alleviate dizzy spells. Continue to drink plenty of water during each week, even if you don't feel thirsty.

Sleep: Getting enough quality sleep is essential for your body and mind. Try to establish a good sleep pattern and make an effort to wind down before bedtime. Being well rested helps keep stress levels down.

Stress: Managing your stress helps considerably during any point in your journey. Stress impacts the balance of bacteria in your gut and can induce constipation or diarrhea and can disrupt your immune system. When we are stressed, our body releases cortisol, which can slow down the digestion of your food.

Week 2: All Meats, Salt (C2)

WEEK 2	MEAL 1	MEAL 2
MONDAY	Perfect Ground Beef (page 109) with Oven-Cooked Bacon (page 108)	Bone-In Rib Eye (page 56), 1 serving
TUESDAY	Leg of Lamb (page 71), 1 serving	Delicious Sirloin (page 54), 1 serving
WEDNESDAY	Strip Steak (page 55), 1 serving	*Perfect Ground Beef leftovers* with *Oven-Cooked Bacon leftovers*
THURSDAY	Poached Chicken Breast (page 74)	Strip Steak (page 55), 1 serving
FRIDAY	*Poached Chicken Breast leftovers*	Sizzling Salmon (page 93), 1 serving, with Roasted Bone Marrow (page 57)
SATURDAY	Bone-In Rib Eye (page 56), 1 serving, with Crispy Chicken Skins (page 77)	Delicious Sirloin (page 54), 1 serving, with *Roasted Bone Marrow leftovers*
SUNDAY	Sizzling Salmon (page 93), 1 serving	The Naked Burger (page 58), 1 serving

SHOPPING LIST

MEAT AND SEAFOOD

- Bacon, 1 (12-ounce) package
- Bone-in rib eye, 2 (1-pound) steaks
- Chicken breasts, boneless, skin on, 4 (8-ounce) breasts

- Ground 80/20 chuck beef (1½ pounds)
- Lamb leg steak, 1 (1-pound) steak
- Marrow bones (2 pounds)

- Sirloin steaks, 2 (10-ounce) steaks
- Strip steaks, 2 (8-ounce) steaks
- Salmon steaks, skin on, 2 (5-ounce) steaks

PANTRY

- Chicken broth
- Kosher salt

WHAT TO KNOW

Digestion: By week 2, your detox symptoms should be calming down. The transition from keto to carnivore is much kinder to your digestion than if you go from the standard American diet to eating full carnivore.

Appetite: Your appetite will likely decrease in week 2. Listen to your body and try to eat intuitively. You may feel unmotivated to eat much, but I would encourage you to have at least two small meals each day.

Stress: Having a positive mindset will help keep stress levels down this week. Focus on the foods you are enjoying rather than the foods you cannot eat.

Week 3: All Meats, Salt, Eggs, and Low-Sugar Dairy (C3)

WEEK 3	MEAL 1	MEAL 2
MONDAY	Perfect Ground Beef (page 109) with Baked Eggs (page 42), 1 serving	Seared Scallops (page 92), 1 serving, with Oven-Cooked Bacon (page 108)
TUESDAY	Cheese Shells (page 112) with *Perfect Ground Beef leftovers* and sour cream	Chicken Schnitzel (page 79), 1 serving
WEDNESDAY	Lamb Kebabs (page 70) with *Oven-Cooked Bacon leftovers*	Bone-In Rib Eye (page 56), 1 serving
THURSDAY	Baked Eggs (page 42), 1 serving, with *Lamb Kebabs leftovers*	Sizzling Salmon (page 93), 1 serving
FRIDAY	The Naked Burger (page 58), 1 serving, with Chicken Liver Pâté (page 75), 1 serving	The Perfect Omelet (page 41), 1 serving, with *Oven-Cooked Bacon leftovers*
SATURDAY	2 Poached Eggs (page 40), with *Oven-Cooked Bacon leftovers*	Strip Steak (page 55), 1 serving, with sour cream
SUNDAY	Skillet Eggs with Thyme (page 46), 1 serving	Delicious Sirloin (page 54), 1 serving, with sour cream and Parmesan cheese

MEAT AND SEAFOOD

- Bacon, 2 (12-ounce) packages
- Bone-in rib eye (1 pound)
- Chicken breast, boneless, skinless (4 ounces)
- Chicken liver (1 pound)
- Ground 80/20 chuck beef (1½ pounds)
- Lamb leg steak (1 pound)
- Sirloin steak, 1 (10-ounce) steak
- Strip steak, 1 (8-ounce) steak
- Salmon steak, skin on, 1 (5-ounce) steak
- Scallops (½ pound)

DAIRY AND EGGS

- Butter, salted, 1 (1-pound) box
- Cheddar cheese 1 (8-ounce) block
- Eggs (2 dozen)
- Parmesan cheese, 1 (8-ounce) wedge
- Sour cream, 1 (8-ounce) container

PANTRY

- Avocado oil
- Chicken fat
- Kosher salt
- Pepper, black
- Pork rinds

WHAT TO KNOW

Appetite: You can expect to continue a reduction in appetite this week. When I did this plan, I definitely thought less about food throughout the day. I enjoyed the two meals I ate, and I didn't have any cravings in between meals. You should notice that your jeans are a little looser around the waist.

Digestion: With the introduction of new foods this week, pay attention to how you feel. Do any foods make you feel bloated or do you have indigestion? Take notes along the way. Dairy can be something that your body does not tolerate well, so be on the lookout for that this week in particular.

Sleep: Continue with your healthy sleep habits. Now that your body is getting used to eating carnivore, you should enjoy a restful night's sleep and wake up full of energy.

Week 4: All Meats, Salt, Eggs, and Low-Sugar Dairy, Spices, and Condiments (C4)

WEEK 4	MEAL 1	MEAL 2
MONDAY	Baked Eggs (page 42), 1 serving, with Oven-Cooked Bacon (page 108)	Leg of Lamb (page 71)
TUESDAY	Meat Lover's Scramble (page 43)	The Naked Burger (page 58), 1 serving, with *Oven-Cooked Bacon leftovers*
WEDNESDAY	Blackened Cod (page 94), 1 serving, with sour cream	*Meat Lover's Scramble leftovers*
THURSDAY	Panfried Tilapia with Garlic and Lemon (page 96), 1 serving	Slow-Cooked Chuck (page 59) with Baked Eggs (page 42)
FRIDAY	*Slow-Cooked Chuck leftovers* with *Baked Eggs Leftovers*	Chicken Schnitzel (page 79), 1 serving
SATURDAY	Fried Cod with Parmesan Crust (page 95), 1 serving	Whole Roast Chicken (page 76) with Queso (page 113)
SUNDAY	Skillet Eggs with Thyme (page 46), 1 serving, with *Whole Roast Chicken leftovers*	Garlic and Mustard Strip Steak (page 60), 1 serving

SHOPPING LIST

MEAT AND SEAFOOD

- Bacon, 1 (12-ounce) package
- Bacon bits, 1 (3-ounce) jar
- Chicken breast, boneless, skinless (4 ounces)
- Chicken, whole, 1 (6-pound) chicken
- Chuck steak (2½ pounds)
- Ground 80/20 chuck beef (1 pound)
- Ham, deli (4 ounces)
- Lamb leg steak (1 pound)
- Strip steak, 1 (1-pound) steak
- Cod loin, skinless, boneless, 2 (½-pound) fillets
- Tilapia, 1 (½-pound) fillet

DAIRY AND EGGS

- Butter, salted, 1 (1-pound) box
- Cheddar cheese, 1 (8-ounce) wedge
- Cream cheese, 1 (8-ounce) package
- Cream, heavy, 1 (1-pint) carton
- Eggs (2 dozen)
- Parmesan cheese, 1 (8-ounce) wedge
- Sour cream (8 ounces)

PRODUCE

- Garlic (1 bulb)
- Lemons (2)
- Lime (1)
- Onion (1)
- Parsley, fresh (1 bunch)
- Rosemary, fresh (1 bunch)
- Thyme, fresh (1 bunch)

PANTRY

- Avocado oil
- Balsamic vinegar
- Basil, dried
- Beef broth
- Garlic, dried minced
- Garlic powder
- Ginger, ground
- Kosher salt
- Mustard powder
- Olive oil
- Olive oil spray
- Onion, dried minced
- Onion powder
- Oregano, dried
- Oregano, ground
- Paprika
- Pepper, black
- Pork rinds
- Rosemary, dried
- Thyme, dried
- Thyme, ground

WHAT TO KNOW

Appetite: Pay attention to your appetite this week. The reset planner is a guide. Try to eat only when you are hungry and stop when you feel full. I had to be mindful of this, as I was so excited to have new food choices each week that I was tempted to eat more than I needed.

Digestion: Continue to make notes if any foods you eat this week cause inflammation. You may find that you digest certain foods better than others.

Energy: Enjoy all this new-found energy and expend it in daily exercise. This was the week that I really killed it at the gym.

Week 5: Clean Keto (CK)

WEEK 5	MEAL 1	MEAL 2
MONDAY	Salmon Fritters (page 99) with Tartar Sauce (page 129)	Strip Steak (page 55), 1 serving, with Queso (page 113)
TUESDAY	Cheese Shells (page 112), 1 serving, with Perfect Ground Beef (page 109) and *Queso leftovers*	The Naked Burger (page 58), 1 serving, with ½ avocado
WEDNESDAY	Baked Eggs (page 42), 1 serving, with *Perfect Ground Beef leftovers* and *Queso leftovers*	Lemon and Garlic Asparagus (page 116), 1 serving, with, *Salmon Fritters leftovers*
THURSDAY	Ham and Brie Frittata (page 45) with whole-grain mustard	Bone-In Rib Eye (page 56), 1 serving, with *Queso leftovers* and ½ avocado

WEEK 5	MEAL 1	MEAL 2
FRIDAY	Lamb Kebabs (page 70) with Mozzarella Bites (page 114), 1 serving	*Ham and Brie Frittata leftovers* with Oven-Cooked Bacon (page 108)
SATURDAY	Tomato and Basil Meatballs (page 64) with Cauliflower Rice (page 117)	*Lamb Kebabs leftovers* with *Oven-Cooked Bacon leftovers* and ½ avocado
SUNDAY	Herby Chicken Omelet (page 47), 1 serving	*Tomato and Basil Meatballs leftovers* with *Cauliflower Rice leftovers*

SHOPPING LIST

MEAT

- Bacon, 1 (12-ounce) package
- Bone-in rib eye, 1 (1-pound) steak
- Chicken, cooked (2 ounces)
- Ground 80/20 chuck beef (2½ pounds)
- Ham, deli (2 ounces)
- Lamb leg steak (1 pound)
- Strip steak, 1 (8-ounce) steak

DAIRY AND EGGS

- Brie (4 ounces)
- Butter, salted, 1 (1-pound) box
- Cheddar cheese, 2 (8-ounce) blocks
- Cream cheese (8 ounces)
- Cream, heavy (1 quart)
- Eggs (2 dozen)
- Mozzarella cheese, 2 (8-ounce) blocks
- Parmesan cheese, 1 (8-ounce) wedge

PRODUCE

- Almond flour
- Asparagus (1 bunch)
- Avocados (2)
- Basil, fresh (1 bunch)
- Carrots, 1 (1-pound) bag
- Cauliflower rice, 2 (10-ounce) bags
- Celery (1 bunch)
- Garlic (1 bulb)
- Jalapeño pepper, fresh (1)
- Lemons (2)
- Lime (1)
- Onion (1)
- Parsley, fresh (1 bunch)
- Salmon, boneless, canned, 3 (5-ounce) cans
- Scallions (1 bunch)
- Spinach, baby, 1 (5-ounce) package
- Tomatoes (4)

PANTRY

- Avocado oil mayonnaise
- Avocado oil spray
- Basil, dried
- Beef broth
- Chicken broth
- Dill, dried
- Dill pickles
- Garlic, dried minced
- Garlic powder
- Kosher salt
- Lemon pepper
- Mustard, yellow
- Mustard, whole-grain
- Olive oil
- Olive oil spray
- Onion powder
- Oregano, dried
- Paprika
- Parsley, dried
- Pepper, black
- Rosemary, dried
- Soy sauce
- Thyme, dried
- Thyme, ground
- Tomato ketchup, low-sugar
- Tomato paste
- Tomato sauce
- Vinegar, white wine
- Worcestershire sauce

WHAT TO KNOW

Appetite: This week is the first step toward your new, clean keto lifestyle. It will be a test to see if you enjoy clean keto rather than carnivore and, more importantly, how your body responds.

Digestion: With the introduction of a keto approach to food this week, be especially mindful of how you feel. How do these foods impact your digestion and overall well-being?

Energy: It will be interesting to see how introducing more carbs this week affects your energy levels and overall mood. Pay attention to this and adjust next week's reset plan to suit your needs. You may prefer to stay closer to carnivore.

Week 6: Clean Keto (CK)

WEEK 6	MEAL 1	MEAL 2
MONDAY	Skillet Eggs with Thyme (page 46), 1 serving, with Oven-Cooked Bacon (page 108), 1 serving	Crab-Stuffed Portobello Mushrooms (page 104), 1 serving, with Loaded Sour Cream (page 130)
TUESDAY	Citrus-Ginger Crab Cakes (page 98) with Tartar Sauce (page 129)	Braised Oxtail (page 65), 1 serving
WEDNESDAY	Tilapia Bisque (page 105)	Perfect Pork Chops (page 68), 1 serving, with Lemon and Garlic Asparagus (page 116), 1 serving
THURSDAY	Garlic and Herb Pork Loin Chop (page 69), 1 serving, with *Loaded Sour Cream leftovers*	*Citrus-Ginger Crab Cakes leftovers* with *Tartar Sauce leftovers*
FRIDAY	*Tilapia Bisque leftovers*	Delicious Sirloin (page 54), 1 serving, with Dill Dip (page 115)
SATURDAY	Shrimp Salad (page 101) with Mozzarella Bites (page 114), 1 serving	Braised Short Ribs (page 62) with Lyonnaise Faux-tatoes (page 118)
SUNDAY	*Braised Short Ribs leftovers* with *Lyonnaise Faux-tatoes leftovers*	Blackened Cod (page 94), 1 serving, with *Tartar Sauce leftovers*

SHOPPING LIST

MEAT

- Bacon, 1 (12-ounce) package
- Oxtail (1 pound)
- Pork chop, bone-in, 1 (11-ounce) chop
- Pork loin, boneless (3 ounces)
- Short ribs, boneless (1½ pounds)
- Top sirloin steak, 1 (10-ounce) steak

SEAFOOD

- Crab claw meat (2 ounces)
- Crabmeat, lump (1 pound)
- Cod loin, 1 (½-pound) fillet
- Shrimp, shelled and deveined (1 pound)
- Tilapia, 1 (½-pound) fillet

EGGS AND DAIRY

- Butter, salted, 1 (1-pound) box
- Cheddar cheese, 1 (8-ounce) block
- Cream cheese (8 ounces)
- Cream, heavy (1 pint)
- Eggs (half dozen)
- Mozzarella cheese, 1 (8-ounce) block
- Parmesan cheese, 1 (8-ounce) wedge
- Sour cream (16 ounces)

PRODUCE

- Asparagus (1 bunch)
- Basil, fresh (1 bunch)
- Carrots, 1 (1-pound) bag
- Celery (1 bunch)
- Dill, fresh (1 bunch)
- Garlic (2 bulbs)
- Grapefruit (1)
- Jalapeño pepper (1)
- Lemons (3)
- Lime (1)
- Mushroom, portobello (1)
- Mushrooms (of choice), 1 (8-ounce) package
- Onions (3)
- Parsley, fresh (1 bunch)
- Radishes (1 bunch)
- Rosemary, fresh (1 bunch)
- Rutabaga (1)
- Scallions (1 bunch)
- Spinach, baby, 1 (5-ounce) package
- Thyme, fresh (1 bunch)

PANTRY

- Avocado oil
- Avocado oil mayonnaise
- Avocado oil spray
- Banana pepper
- Beef broth
- Cayenne pepper
- Chicken broth
- Dill, dried
- Dill pickles
- Garlic, dried minced
- Garlic powder
- Ginger, ground
- Kosher salt
- Lemon pepper
- Olive oil
- Olive oil spray
- Onion, dried minced
- Onion powder
- Oregano, dried
- Oregano, ground
- Paprika
- Pepper, black
- Pork rinds
- Rosemary, dried
- Soy sauce
- Thyme, dried
- Thyme, ground
- Tomato paste
- Turmeric, ground
- Worcestershire sauce

WHAT TO KNOW

Appetite: If you find that you want more food this week, pay attention to the nutritional value of what you are eating. Make sure that you eat plenty of meals.

Digestion: This week was the week I realized that keto carnivore (specifically, the recipes that fall under C4) was the best approach for my body. I noticed that my appetite grew and my energy levels dropped when I added more carbs. Everybody is different and you may find that keto is the best fit for you.

Moving Forward: Once you have worked through the 6-week reset plan and have discovered which phase works best for you, use the classifications (C1 to C4 and CK) to personalize your own reset plans going forward.

Kitchen Essentials

These are the kitchen essentials needed for cooking the recipes in this book.

- Avocado oil (and spray)
- Baking sheet
- Cast-iron pan
- Chicken fat
- Coconut oil (and spray)
- Dutch oven
- Food thermometer
- Grass-fed butter, salted
- Lard
- Measuring cups and spoons
- Mixing spoons
- Muffin pan
- Nonstick frying pan
- Oils
- Olive oil (and spray)
- Saucepans
- Silicone mat
- Spatula, narrow-ended
- Spatula, wide-ended
- Tallow

Pantry Essentials

If you keep an array of herbs, spices, and a few other commonly used ingredients in the pantry, you'll always be ready to make any of the recipes in this book.

- Allulose
- Almond flour
- Avocado oil mayonnaise
- Baking powder
- Beef broth
- Cayenne pepper
- Chicken broth
- Dill, dried
- Garlic

- Garlic, dried minced
- Ginger, ground
- Italian seasoning
- Kosher salt
- Lemon pepper
- Onion, dried minced
- Onion powder
- Oregano
- Paprika
- Pepper, black

- Pork rinds
- Soy sauce
- Thyme, dried
- Tomato paste
- Tomato sauce
- Turmeric
- Worcestershire sauce
- Xanthan gum

PART 2

75 Recipes

The Perfect Omelet, page 41

Breakfast

C3, C4, CK

Poached Eggs

PREP TIME: 5 minutes | **COOK TIME:** 10 minutes | **SERVES 2**

Eggs are incredibly nutritious and full of good fats and protein. They will become a featured star in your diet, whether you are keto or carnivore. Learning different ways to cook them will keep things interesting. Poaching eggs may seem daunting if you haven't done it before, but once you make them a couple of times, you'll see how easy they are.

2 cups water

1 tablespoon vinegar
   (optional)

4 eggs, cold

½ teaspoon kosher salt

1. In a small saucepan, combine the water and vinegar (if using) and bring to a boil over high heat. Reduce the heat to medium to bring the water to a simmer.

2. Crack an egg into a separate ramekin or measuring cup.

3. Using a spatula, swirl the water in one direction, and carefully drop the egg into the center of the swirl. Crack each of the remaining 3 eggs, one at a time, into the ramekin, then drop each one into the swirling water.

4. Cook until the yolks are semisoft, 2 or 3 minutes. For a firmer yolk, cook them for 3 or 4 minutes.

5. Using a slotted spoon, transfer the eggs to plates. Sprinkle with salt and serve.

TIP: For a boost of extra flavor, add a sprinkle of Everything Bagel Spice Blend (page 127).

PER SERVING (2 EGGS): FAT 60%; PROTEIN 38%; CARBS 2%; Calories: 143; Total fat: 10g; Protein: 13g; Total carbs: 1g; Fiber: 0g; Net carbs: 1g; Sodium: 433mg; Iron: 2mg

C3, C4, CK

The Perfect Omelet

PREP TIME: 5 minutes | **COOK TIME:** 10 minutes | **SERVES 2**

Making an omelet is a great skill to have, and with this recipe there's no tricky flipping involved. I learned this technique when I was newly married, and I've never looked back. It creates a perfect omelet every time. If you're eating in a later phase, add your favorite shredded cheese or cooked fillings before folding the omelet over.

2 tablespoons salted butter
4 eggs
1 egg yolk
½ teaspoon kosher salt
Freshly ground black pepper

1. In a small, nonstick frying pan, melt the butter over medium heat.

2. In a small bowl, whisk together the eggs, egg yolk, salt, and pepper to taste, and pour the mixture into the pan.

3. Cook for 1 minute. Using a spatula, gently push the cooked edges inward and tip the pan so the uncooked egg fills the space you have created.

4. Continue this process around the edges of the omelet and repeat three or four times, until the surface of the egg is almost cooked. Using the spatula, fold the omelet in half.

5. Cook for 1 minute, turn the omelet over, and cook for 1 minute more. Cut the omelet in half and divide between two plates. Serve immediately.

PER SERVING: FAT 76%; PROTEIN 22%; CARBS 2%;
Calories: 272; Total fat: 23g; Protein: 14g; Total carbs: 1g;
Fiber: 0g; Net carbs: 1g; Sodium: 528mg; Iron: 2mg

C3, C4, CK

Baked Eggs

PREP TIME: 5 minutes | **COOK TIME:** 20 minutes | **SERVES 2**

Boiling and peeling eggs can be frustrating and time-consuming, so I consider this recipe to be an essential life hack! Baking your eggs this way is foolproof, quick, and creates little mess. And the best part? They provide a delicious high-protein meal. Eat them on their own or serve them as a side to accompany another meal.

Olive oil spray, for greasing
4 eggs
1 teaspoon kosher salt
½ teaspoon freshly ground black pepper

1. Preheat the oven to 350°F. Grease a four-cup, nonstick muffin tin with olive oil spray.

2. Crack an egg into each of the muffin cups. Season with salt and pepper.

3. Bake for 14 minutes for a runny yolk or 18 minutes for a firmer yolk.

TIP: For a boost of extra flavor, add a sprinkle of Italian Spice Blend (page 126).

PER SERVING (2 EGGS): FAT 59%; PROTEIN 38%; CARBS 3%; Calories: 145; Total fat: 10g; Protein: 13g; Total carbs: 1g; Fiber: 0g; Net carbs: 1g; Sodium: 723mg; Iron: 2mg

C3, C4, CK

Meat Lover's Scramble

PREP TIME: 10 minutes | **COOK TIME:** 10 Minutes | **SERVES 2**

This hearty and filling scramble is packed with protein and flavor. You can vary it by switching the seasonings for different flavors or trying different protein combinations. Add grated cheese for a boost in fat and flavor.

7 ounces 80/20 ground chuck beef

½ teaspoon garlic powder

½ teaspoon paprika

½ teaspoon Italian Spice Blend (page 126)

½ teaspoon onion powder

4 large eggs

2 egg yolks

2 tablespoons heavy cream

½ teaspoon kosher salt

½ teaspoon freshly ground black pepper

2 tablespoons salted butter

¼ cup cooked bacon bits

¼ cup diced ham

1. In a small, nonstick frying pan, cook the ground beef over medium-high heat, using a spatula to break up the meat, until it's cooked through, 3 or 4 minutes.

2. Add the garlic, paprika, Italian spice blend, and onion powder and continue to cook, stirring frequently, until browned. Reduce the heat to medium-low and cook, stirring occasionally, for 15 minutes.

3. While the meat is cooking, in a medium bowl, combine the eggs, egg yolks, and heavy cream, and whisk until fluffy. Add the salt and pepper and whisk until combined.

4. In a medium, nonstick frying pan, melt the butter over medium-low heat. Add the egg mixture to the pan and, using a spatula, begin to move the egg mixture around the pan, drawing the cooked mixture from the edges into the middle. Keep moving the egg around until it looks about half-cooked. Add the bacon bits and ham and continue to scramble.

5. Using a slotted spoon, add the ground beef to the scramble and continue to cook until the egg looks cooked; 2 or 3 minutes. Serve hot.

PER SERVING: FAT 73%; PROTEIN 24%; CARBS 3%; Calories: 702; Total fat: 58g; Protein: 40g; Total carbs: 4g; Fiber: 1g; Net carbs: 3g; Sodium: 1031mg; Iron: 5mg

C4, CK

Eggs-cellent Muffins

PREP TIME: 10 minutes | **COOK TIME:** 15 Minutes | **MAKES 4 MUFFINS**

I absolutely love this gem of a recipe. These wonderful muffins can of course be eaten any time of the day and enjoyed hot or cold. They are extremely versatile, since you can add other ingredients, such as cheese, if you want to. They travel well as a snack and keep for a couple of days in the refrigerator if you have leftovers.

Olive oil spray, for greasing

4 eggs

2 tablespoons heavy cream

1 teaspoon kosher salt

½ teaspoon freshly ground
   black pepper

½ teaspoon onion powder

¼ cup grated
   mozzarella cheese

2 ounces cooked chicken
   breast, shredded

1. Preheat the oven to 400°F. Grease a four-cup muffin tin with olive oil spray.

2. In a small bowl, whisk together the eggs, cream, salt, pepper, and onion powder.

3. Pour the egg mixture equally into the four cups.

4. Bake for 3 minutes. Divide the cheese and chicken equally into each cup.

5. Bake for 12 or 13 minutes more, depending on how brown you like the top of your muffins.

TIP: These muffins are easily customized. Try adding Buffalo Cheddar cheese and garlic for some bigger flavors. For stricter carnivores, omit the onion powder.

PER SERVING (2 MUFFINS): FAT 60%; PROTEIN 37%; CARBS 3%;
Calories: 144; Total fat: 10g; Protein: 12g; Total carbs: 1g;
Fiber: 0g; Net carbs: 1g; Sodium: 419mg; Iron: 1mg

Ham and Brie Frittata

PREP TIME: 10 minutes | **COOK TIME:** 20 minutes | **SERVES 4**

Choose your favorite meats and cheeses to customize this dish, although this combination of ham, Brie, and mustard works particularly well together. Enjoy it for breakfast, lunch, or dinner. It is delicious served hot or cold and will keep for up to 2 days in the refrigerator.

Olive oil spray, for greasing
6 eggs
4 egg yolks
¼ cup heavy cream
1 teaspoon kosher salt
1 teaspoon freshly ground black pepper
2 teaspoons whole-grain mustard
4 ounces Brie, cut into cubes
2 ounces deli ham, diced

1. Preheat the oven to 400°F. Grease a 9-inch round baking dish with olive oil spray.

2. In a large bowl, whisk together the eggs, egg yolks, cream, salt, pepper, and mustard. Pour the mixture into the baking dish.

3. Bake for 5 minutes.

4. Remove the dish from the oven and carefully scatter the Brie and ham as evenly as possible over the top.

5. Bake for 12 to 14 minutes, or until the frittata begins to brown. Leave the frittata to cool for a few minutes, then cut slices directly from the dish.

TIP: To make this a C3 carnivore dish, omit the mustard and black pepper.

PER SERVING: FAT 70%; PROTEIN 27%; CARBS 3%; Calories: 325; Total fat: 25g; Protein: 21g; Total carbs: 2g; Fiber: 0g; Net carbs: 2g; Sodium: 796mg; Iron: 2mg

Skillet Eggs with Thyme

PREP TIME: 5 minutes | **COOK TIME:** 10 minutes | **SERVES 2**

Skillet eggs are satisfying to make, and they look so pretty cooked in a cast-iron pan. But you can make this in any pan you have. They'll come out just as good. I use a mixture of butter and oil to cook the egg because it regulates the temperature of the butter and keeps it from burning.

1 tablespoon olive oil

1 tablespoon salted butter

4 eggs

½ teaspoon kosher salt

¼ teaspoon freshly ground black pepper

1 sprig fresh thyme

1. In a medium, cast-iron pan or nonstick frying pan, melt the oil and butter over medium heat until they begin to sizzle.

2. Carefully crack each egg into the skillet, making sure not to break the yolks. Sprinkle the salt and pepper over the eggs and place the thyme sprig on top.

3. Reduce the heat to low, cover, and cook for 1½ minutes for runny eggs or 2½ minutes for a firmer yolk. Remove the thyme sprig and serve immediately.

PER SERVING (2 EGGS): FAT 77%; PROTEIN 22%; CARBS 1%; Calories: 254; Total fat: 22g; Protein: 13g; Total carbs: 1g; Fiber: 0g; Net carbs: 1g; Sodium: 479mg; Iron: 2mg

CK

Herby Chicken Omelet

PREP TIME: 10 minutes | **COOK TIME:** 10 minutes | **SERVES 2**

Eggs definitely don't have to be boring. Cooking in your own kitchen means that you can experiment with all your favorite flavors. This lovely recipe plays with some tasty ingredients and comes together in minutes. The combination of chicken, spinach, and mozzarella is delicious, and the oregano and thyme add a wonderful earthy flavor that pairs beautifully with the chicken.

4 eggs

1 egg yolk

½ teaspoon dried oregano

½ teaspoon ground thyme

1 teaspoon kosher salt

½ teaspoon freshly ground black pepper

2 tablespoons salted butter

⅓ cup grated mozzarella cheese

6 baby spinach leaves

2 ounces cooked chicken, shredded

1. In a medium bowl, whisk together the eggs, egg yolk, oregano, thyme, salt, and pepper.

2. In a nonstick frying pan, melt the butter over medium heat. Add the egg mixture and let it cook for 1 minute. Sprinkle the cheese, spinach, and chicken over the omelet.

3. Reduce the heat to medium-low, cover, and cook until the eggs have set, 3 or 4 minutes.

4. Cut the omelet into two equal pieces, slide them onto individual plates, and enjoy.

TIP: Add some pickled jalapeño peppers at the end if you'd like a little heat.

PER SERVING: FAT 67%; PROTEIN 30%; CARBS 3%; Calories: 381; Total fat: 29g; Protein: 27g; Total carbs: 3g; Fiber: 1g; Net carbs: 2g; Sodium: 973mg; Iron: 4mg

Avocado Scramble

PREP TIME: 10 minutes | **COOK TIME:** 10 minutes | **SERVES 2**

This scramble is a very easy way to make eggs, even for those who don't cook much. It's a simple recipe, and since everything is cooked together, it's nearly impossible to mess it up. Serve it for a classic breakfast or eat it as a snack or even for lunch or dinner. Leftovers can be refrigerated overnight and you'll have a heat-and-eat meal ready to go for the next day.

4 large eggs

2 egg yolks

1 teaspoon kosher salt

½ teaspoon freshly ground
  black pepper

1 teaspoon onion powder

2 tablespoons salted butter

¼ cup grated
  Cheddar cheese

1 scallion, finely chopped

4 cooked bacon slices,
  crumbled

1 medium avocado, peeled,
  pitted, and cubed

1. In a medium bowl, whisk together the eggs, egg yolks, salt, pepper, and onion powder. Alternatively, you can use an electric hand mixer with a whisk attachment, which will create a fluffier scramble.

2. In a nonstick frying pan, melt the butter over medium heat. Add the eggs and cook for 10 seconds. Using a spatula, begin moving the eggs around the pan. Add the cheese, scallion, and bacon and continue to cook, using the spatula to scramble the eggs, for about 1 minute. Add the avocado and use the spatula to combine all the fillings.

3. Reduce the heat to low and cook until the eggs are cooked to your liking, about 2 minutes more.

TIP: Feel free to add different ingredients such as grated Parmesan or goat cheese, minced fresh rosemary or dried oregano, and diced ham or cooked chicken.

PER SERVING: FAT 74%; PROTEIN 19%; CARBS 7%; Calories: 633; Total fat: 53g; Protein: 29g; Total carbs: 12g; Fiber: 7g; Net carbs: 5g; Sodium: 1311mg; Iron: 3mg

CK

Just-Sweet-Enough Waffles

PREP TIME: 10 minutes | **COOK TIME:** 10 minutes | **MAKES 3 WAFFLES**

My kids love to help me make this quick and easy breakfast treat, which has just the right amount of sweetness. For a larger meal, pair the waffles with some crispy bacon and fried eggs. So good.

2 eggs

¼ teaspoon kosher salt

⅓ cup grated
  mozzarella cheese

2 tablespoons heavy cream

½ teaspoon baking powder

¼ teaspoon ground ginger

¼ teaspoon ground
  cinnamon

¼ teaspoon almond extract

1 tablespoon keto-friendly
  powdered sweetener

1. Turn on the waffle maker to its highest temperature.

2. In a small bowl, whisk together the eggs, salt, cheese, cream, baking powder, ginger, cinnamon, almond extract, and powdered sweetener until frothy.

3. Pour a third of the batter into the waffle maker and cook for 5 minutes, or according to the manufacturer's instructions. Repeat for the remaining two waffles.

TIP: This recipe can also be used to make four crêpes. Pour the batter onto a flat griddle or into a nonstick frying pan and cook on low heat for 3 or 4 minutes per side.

PER SERVING (1 WAFFLE): FAT 71%; PROTEIN 25%; CARBS 4%;
Calories: 121; Total fat: 10g; Protein: 7g; Total carbs: 1g;
Fiber: 0g; Net carbs: 1g; Sodium: 233mg; Iron: 1mg

CK

Savory Waffles with Broccoli Slaw

PREP TIME: 10 minutes | **COOK TIME:** 10 minutes | **MAKES 3 WAFFLES**

This recipe reminds me of hash browns, because it has that wonderful comfort food feeling about it. The waffles taste great on their own for breakfast or as an accompaniment to a protein dish. I always eat mine fresh off the waffle maker, but they are just as tasty reheated the next morning.

2 cups broccoli slaw

1 cup water

1 egg

½ cup grated
   mozzarella cheese

½ cup grated
   Cheddar cheese

1 teaspoon kosher salt

½ teaspoon yellow mustard

1. Turn on the waffle maker to its highest temperature.

2. Place the broccoli slaw and water in a microwave-safe bowl and microwave for 4 minutes. Let cool. Squeeze out the excess liquid with a paper towel.

3. In a medium bowl, whisk together the egg, mozzarella, Cheddar, salt, mustard, and broccoli slaw.

4. Pour a third of the mixture onto the waffle maker and cook for 5 minutes, or according to the manufacturer's instructions. Repeat for the remaining two waffles.

TIP: For a little extra indulgence, add a dollop of sour cream to the mixture. If you don't have a waffle maker, divide the mixture into equal-size patties and cook them with a little oil in a nonstick frying pan for 2 to 3 minutes per side.

PER SERVING (1 WAFFLE): FAT 62%; PROTEIN 28%; CARBS 10%; Calories: 177; Total fat: 12g; Protein: 13g; Total carbs: 5g; Fiber: 2g; Net carbs: 3g; Sodium: 679mg; Iron: 1mg

CK

Ginger Muffins

PREP TIME: 15 minutes | **COOK TIME:** 20 minutes | **MAKES 6 MUFFINS**

These breakfast muffins have a nice amount of sweetness, which is balanced with a delicious nutty flavor. They will keep in an airtight container for up to 5 days and can be frozen for up to 2 months. Be sure to have all the ingredients at room temperature, as it will affect the baking time.

Olive oil spray, for greasing

2 eggs, at room temperature

¼ cup coconut oil, at room temperature

¼ cup (½ stick) salted butter, at room temperature

¼ cup granular erythritol or another keto sweetener

2 teaspoons brown sugar erythritol

½ teaspoon almond extract

½ cup almond flour

¼ cup coconut flour

1 teaspoon baking powder

½ teaspoon ground ginger

½ teaspoon xanthan gum

¼ cup chopped pecans

2 tablespoons sunflower seeds

2 tablespoons pumpkin seeds

1 teaspoon chia seeds

1. Preheat the oven to 350°F. Grease a six-cup muffin tin with olive oil spray, or use a six-cup silicone muffin pan.

2. In a large bowl, whisk together the eggs, coconut oil, butter, granular erythritol, brown sugar erythritol, and almond extract.

3. Add the almond flour, coconut flour, baking powder, ginger, and xanthan gum and mix with a spoon until the ingredients are combined.

4. Add the pecans, sunflower seeds, pumpkin seeds, and chia seeds and stir until combined.

5. Using an ice cream scoop or a large serving spoon, divide the mixture equally into the muffin tin.

6. Bake for 16 minutes, or until the muffins are golden on top and a toothpick inserted into the middle comes out clean without any batter on it.

7. Let the muffins cool on a wire rack.

TIP: Always let keto baked goods cool completely before eating. As they cool, the texture will become firmer.

PER SERVING (1 MUFFIN): FAT 83%; PROTEIN 9%; CARBS 8%; Calories: 307; Total fat: 30g; Protein: 7g; Total carbs: 6g; Fiber: 3g; Net carbs: 3g; Sodium: 93mg; Iron: 2mg

Delicious Sirloin, 54

Beef and Other Ruminants

Delicious Sirloin

PREP TIME: 1 minute | **COOK TIME:** 10 minutes | **SERVES 2**

When you make this recipe, you'll learn how to use the fat within the meat to create more flavor, and you can use that skill for any meat you cook. Sirloin is a great cut to choose, as it's easy to cook. There are no bones to navigate, and the fat within the cut delivers on taste. The cooked steak can be refrigerated overnight. To reheat, bring the steak to room temperature and then panfry it for 1 minute per side until heated through. Experiment with herbs like rosemary for some extra flavor.

2 (10-ounce) grass-fed top sirloin steaks (about 1-inch thick)

2 teaspoons kosher salt

1. Pat dry each steak with paper towels and season on both sides with the salt, making sure to rub the salt into the steak. Let rest for 30 minutes.

2. Heat a cast-iron pan over medium-high heat. Place the steaks in the pan and sear for about 2 minutes. Turn the steaks over and sear the other sides for about 2 minutes.

3. Turn the steaks over one more time and cook for 2½ or 3 minutes more for medium-rare, 5 to 7 minutes more for medium, or 8 to 10 minutes more for medium-well.

4. Transfer the steaks to a cutting board and cover them loosely with aluminum foil. Let rest for 10 minutes.

5. Serve whole, or cut the steaks into slices.

TIP: If you have moved past C2 and can include butter and seasonings, cook the steak in 3 tablespoons of butter and 1 tablespoon of avocado oil. Combine 2 teaspoons of Italian Spice Blend (page 126) with the salt and rub that into the steaks before cooking.

PER SERVING: FAT 53%; PROTEIN 47%; CARBS 0%; Calories: 536; Total fat: 32g; Protein: 59g; Total carbs: 0g; Fiber: 0g; Net carbs: 0g; Sodium: 1313mg; Iron: 4mg

C1, C2, C3, C4, CK

Strip Steak

PREP TIME: 2 minutes | **COOK TIME:** 10 minutes | **SERVES 2**

Strip steak, also called top loin, is a popular cut of meat, probably because it's more affordable than filet mignon and is packed with delicious flavor. The beautiful marbling that runs through this steak lends itself perfectly to skillet cooking.

2 (8-ounce) strip steaks

2 teaspoons kosher salt

1. Pat dry each steak and rub the salt over each side.

2. Let the steaks rest at room temperature for 30 minutes before cooking.

3. Heat a cast-iron pan over high heat.

4. Using tongs to hold the steaks, sear the fat strip that runs down one side for 3 minutes. If either strip of fat is more than a ½-inch thick, sear it for 1 minute more. Place the steaks in the pan and cook for 4 minutes. Turn the steaks over and cook them for 4 minutes more. Check the internal temperature of the steaks: 125°F for rare, 135°F for medium-rare, 145°F for medium, 155°F for medium-well.

5. Transfer the steaks to a cutting board, cover them loosely with aluminum foil, and let rest for 10 minutes.

6. Cut the steaks into slices and serve.

TIP: This cut of steak is very flavorful as is, but you can add black pepper and other seasonings if you are looking for more flavor variety. To increase your fat count, add butter to the steak as it is resting.

PER SERVING: FAT 51%; PROTEIN 49%; CARBS 0%; Calories: 429; Total fat: 25g; Protein: 47g; Total carbs: 0g; Fiber: 0g; Net carbs: 0g; Sodium: 1283mg; Iron: 3mg

C1, C2, C3, C4, CK

Bone-In Rib Eye

PREP TIME: 2 minutes | **COOK TIME:** 10 minutes | **SERVES 2**

Glorious rib eye. It is often referred to as the steak-lover's steak, and it's easy to see why. Both the marbling and the inclusion of the bone give rib eye a delicious flavor. Try to choose a steak that has even marbling throughout, which helps keep the steak tender.

2 (1-pound) bone-in rib
eye steaks

2 teaspoons kosher salt

1. Pat the steaks dry with a paper towel and season both sides with salt, making sure to rub it into the meat. Let rest for 30 minutes.

2. Heat a large, cast-iron pan over high heat. Place the steaks in the pan and cook for 5 minutes without moving them. Turn the steaks over and cook for 4 minutes more for medium-rare. Use a meat thermometer to check the internal temperature: 125°F for rare, 135°F for medium-rare, 145°F for medium, 155°F for medium-well.

3. Transfer the steaks to a cutting board, cover them loosely with aluminum foil, and let rest for 10 minutes.

TIP: If you are using spices, feel free to add 1 teaspoon of minced garlic and 1 teaspoon of paprika.

PER SERVING: FAT 57%; PROTEIN 43%; CARBS 0%; Calories: 820; Total fat: 52g; Protein: 88g; Total carbs: 0g; Fiber: 0g; Net carbs: 0g; Sodium: 1324mg; Iron: 12mg

C1, C2, C3, C4, CK

Roasted Bone Marrow

PREP TIME: 5 minutes | **COOK TIME:** 20 minutes | **SERVES 2**

Marrow is one of the simplest meals to make, and it's so good for you. The fat that comes from ruminants is nutrient-dense and can boost your immune system. It is difficult to know how much marrow will come from each bone, so make more than you need and refrigerate the leftovers for up to 3 days. Use a spoon to scoop out the marrow, and if you like, you can freeze the bones for up to 3 months and use them to make bone broth.

2 cups water

1 tablespoon kosher salt

2 pounds marrow bones

1. Preheat the oven to 450°F.

2. In a large bowl, combine the water and salt and mix until the salt is dissolved.

3. Place the bones in the salty water and clean them by rubbing them gently.

4. Pat the bones dry with a paper towel and place them in a roasting pan. If the bones are cut crosswise, place them standing up; if they are cut lengthwise, place them in the pan marrow-side up.

5. Roast for 20 minutes. Serve immediately.

PER SERVING: FAT 63%; PROTEIN 37%; CARBS 0%; Calories: 619; Total fat: 42g; Protein: 51g; Total carbs: 0g; Fiber: 0g; Net carbs: 0g; Sodium: 865mg; Iron: 6mg

C4, CK

The Naked Burger

PREP TIME: 5 minutes | **COOK TIME:** 10 minutes | **SERVES 2**

I think this is possibly the best burger you will ever have. And it is definitely the easiest to prepare. Use a good-quality 80/20 beef because a higher fat content gives the best flavor. Form the burger patties with ground beef straight from the fridge. You want to cook them when they are as cold as possible. Avoid overhandling the meat, or you may end up with a tough burger, and no one wants that.

1 pound 80/20 ground chuck beef

2 teaspoons kosher salt

1 teaspoon freshly ground black pepper

1 tablespoon olive oil

1. Working quickly, form two patties with the ground beef, each one roughly ¾-inch thick. Use your thumb to make an indentation in the middle of each patty and season both sides with the salt and pepper.

2. In a cast-iron pan, heat the olive oil over high heat until it begins to smoke. Add the burgers, making sure to leave space between them, and cook them for 4 or 5 minutes per side for medium rare, or 5 or 6 minutes per side for medium. Use a food thermometer as you are cooking to monitor the temperature: 145°F for medium-rare or 160°F for medium.

3. Transfer the burgers to a plate and let rest for a few minutes before serving.

TIP: To enjoy this burger in week 1 of the reset, omit the black pepper and olive oil.

PER SERVING: FAT 74%; PROTEIN 26%; CARBS 0%; Calories: 639; Total fat: 52g; Protein: 39g; Total carbs: 0g; Fiber: 0g; Net carbs: 0g; Sodium: 1312mg; Iron: 5mg

Slow-Cooked Chuck

PREP TIME: 5 minutes | **COOK TIME:** 5½ hours plus 30 minutes resting time | **SERVES 4**

Chuck is inexpensive, tastes fantastic, and is extremely adaptable. Because it's slow cooked, the meat practically melts in your mouth.

2 teaspoons kosher salt

1 teaspoon freshly ground black pepper

1 teaspoon paprika

1 teaspoon garlic powder

1 (2½-pound) chuck steak

2 tablespoons olive oil

2½ cups beef bone broth, plus more as needed

2 sprigs fresh thyme

1 sprig fresh rosemary

1. Preheat the oven to 275°F.

2. In a small bowl, mix together the salt, pepper, paprika, and garlic powder. Rub the salt mixture over both sides of the steak.

3. In a Dutch oven, heat the olive oil over medium-high heat.

4. Place the steak in the Dutch oven and sear for 5 minutes per side.

5. Pour the bone broth into the Dutch oven, making sure that the liquid reaches at least halfway up the steak. Add more if needed. Place the thyme and rosemary sprigs on top of the meat.

6. Cover the Dutch oven and cook for 5 hours. Check occasionally to make sure that the level of broth is still covering half the steak, and add more broth if necessary.

7. Remove the Dutch oven from the oven. Let the steak rest in the Dutch oven, covered, for 30 minutes. Using two dinner forks, shred the steak while it is still in the pot. The meat should easily fall apart.

TIP: For a fun serving option in week 5 or later, make lettuce boats and top them with the meat, shredded mozzarella, and mustard.

PER SERVING: FAT 69%; PROTEIN 30%; CARBS 1%; Calories: 709; Total fat: 55g; Protein: 54g; Total carbs: 1g; Fiber: 0g; Net carbs: 1g; Sodium: 770mg; Iron: 6mg

Garlic and Mustard Strip Steak

PREP TIME: 10 minutes | **COOK TIME:** 20 minutes | **SERVES 2**

Once you know the best way to cook a strip steak, the possibilities are endless. I love this recipe because it takes an already tasty cut of meat and elevates it to the next level of deliciousness. The potently flavored sauce is a nice complement to the steak, but you can use it with chicken or fish as well. To reheat the sauce, simply add a drop of water to it and warm it up on the stovetop.

2½ teaspoons mustard powder, divided

2 teaspoons kosher salt

1 teaspoon freshly ground black pepper

2 (1-pound) New York strip steaks

1 tablespoon olive oil

¼ cup water

½ cup beef broth

½ cup heavy cream

2 tablespoons balsamic vinegar

½ tablespoon onion powder

½ tablespoon dried minced garlic

¼ cup grated Parmesan cheese

1. In a small bowl, mix together 2 teaspoons of mustard powder, the salt, and pepper.

2. Pat the steaks dry with paper towels and rub the mustard mixture onto both sides.

3. In a cast-iron pan, heat the olive oil over high heat until it begins to smoke, 3 or 4 minutes. Using tongs to hold the steaks, sear the edges with the fat for 3 minutes. Place the steaks flat and cook for 4 minutes.

4. Turn the steaks over and cook for 4 minutes more for medium-rare. Check the internal temperature: 135°F for medium-rare; 145°F for medium. Cook longer for your desired level of doneness.

5. Transfer the steaks to a platter, tent them with aluminum foil, and let rest for 30 minutes.

6. Add the water to the skillet and deglaze the pan over medium-high heat, scraping up any browned bits with a spatula. Let cook until most of the liquid is evaporated.

7. Reduce the heat to medium and add the broth, cream, balsamic vinegar, and the remaining ½ teaspoon of mustard powder to the pan. Cook until the mixture begins to simmer. Add the onion powder, garlic, and Parmesan and whisk until combined.

8. Simmer, whisking occasionally, until the sauce is thickened, about 10 minutes.

9. Cut the steak into slices (removing the fat) and add it to the sauce. Cook until heated through, about 1 minute.

TIP: Pair this recipe with Lyonnaise Faux-tatoes (page 118)

PER SERVING: FAT 66%; PROTEIN 29%; CARBS 5%;
Calories: 1344; Total fat: 98g; Protein: 98g; Total carbs: 12g;
Fiber: 1g; Net carbs: 11g; Sodium: 1560mg; Iron: 9mg

Braised Short Ribs

PREP TIME: 15 minutes | **COOK TIME:** 2½ hours plus 30 minutes resting time | **SERVES 2**

I have chosen to make this recipe with boneless ribs, simply because it offers more meat! To double the amount of protein, use 3 pounds of short ribs. There's no need to alter the amounts of any of the other ingredients. Beware! This dish can produce a fair amount of smoke when you are cooking, so you may want to turn on the oven fan or open a window.

1 teaspoon kosher salt

½ teaspoon freshly ground black pepper

½ teaspoon paprika

1½ pounds boneless short ribs

2 tablespoons olive oil

2 medium celery stalks, roughly chopped

1 medium carrot, roughly chopped

½ small onion, roughly chopped

¼ cup water

2½ cups beef broth

4 garlic cloves, peeled

1 sprig fresh rosemary

1 teaspoon onion powder

1. Preheat the oven to 350°F.

2. In a small bowl, mix together the salt, pepper, and paprika. Pat the short ribs dry with paper towels and rub the mixture all over each one.

3. In a Dutch oven, heat the olive oil over high heat. Place the ribs in the pan and brown for about 1 minute on each side. Transfer the ribs to a plate and set aside.

4. Carefully pour off any excess oil from the Dutch oven. Reduce the heat to medium-high, add the celery, carrots, onion, and water, and cook, deglazing the pan, using a spatula to scrape up any browned bits and stirring, for 5 minutes.

5. Return the short ribs to the pan and pour in the beef broth. The ribs should be three-quarters submerged in the liquid. Add more broth if needed. Add the garlic cloves, rosemary sprig, and onion powder.

6. Cover, transfer the Dutch oven to the oven, and bake for 2 hours. Reduce the heat to 325°F. Check the level of broth and add more if needed. Bake for 30 minutes more.

7. Remove the Dutch oven from the oven. Let the meat rest in the Dutch oven, covered, for 30 minutes. If the sauce seems fatty, skim a little off the top. Remove the rosemary and serve.

TIP: This is an excellent dish to make in advance, as it's easier to skim the hardened fat off the top after it has been refrigerated overnight, and the sauce will have thickened up a little.

PER SERVING: FAT 72%; PROTEIN 24%; CARBS 4%; Calories: 974; Total fat: 79g; Protein: 60g; Total carbs: 9g; Fiber: 2g; Net carbs: 7g; Sodium: 875mg; Iron: 8mg

Tomato and Basil Meatballs

PREP TIME: 20 minutes | **COOK TIME:** 1 hour, 20 minutes | **SERVES 2**

This dish evokes many childhood memories for me. Everyone has their own version of meatballs. This version is mine, and I think it is delicious!

1 egg

¼ cup grated
  Parmesan cheese

1 pound 80/20 ground
  chuck beef

1 tablespoon Italian Spice
  Blend (page 126)

2 tablespoons olive oil

½ small onion,
  finely chopped

2 small celery stalks,
  finely chopped

2 garlic cloves, minced

4 large tomatoes, seeded
  and roughly chopped

4 leaves fresh basil,
  finely chopped

1 teaspoon kosher salt

1 teaspoon freshly ground
  black pepper

1 teaspoon paprika

½ cup tomato sauce

1 tablespoon tomato paste

¾ cup beef broth or
  chicken broth

1. Preheat the oven to 400°F. Line a baking sheet with parchment paper or a silicone mat. Cover a plate with paper towels.

2. In a large bowl, combine the egg, Parmesan, ground beef, and Italian seasoning blend and mix them together using your hands. (I think it's a lot easier doing this step with your hands than with a spoon.)

3. Using your hands, form the mixture into eight equal meatballs. Place them on the baking sheet and bake for 20 minutes. Transfer the meatballs to the prepared plate to remove any excess oil.

4. In a 2-quart saucepan, heat the olive oil over medium heat. Reduce the heat to low, add the onions, celery, and garlic, and sauté for 5 minutes.

5. Add the tomatoes, basil, salt, pepper, paprika, tomato sauce, tomato paste, and beef broth and stir until combined.

6. Add the meatballs to the sauce and gently stir them until they are covered in the sauce.

7. Cover and simmer for 1 hour. Serve immediately.

PER SERVING: FAT 66%; PROTEIN 23%; CARBS 11%; Calories: 924; Total fat: 68g; Protein: 52g; Total carbs: 26g; Fiber: 7g; Net carbs: 19g; Sodium: 763mg; Iron: mg

CK

Braised Oxtail

PREP TIME: 15 minutes | **COOK TIME:** 2 hours | **SERVES 2**

Oxtail used to be considered an offcut, but it provides an incredibly deep flavor in stews and there are many recipes that use it all over the world. Cooked slow and low, the meat gets a rich, comforting flavor and a velvety texture. Fun fact: Oxtail doesn't actually come from an ox, but from a cow!

3 tablespoons olive oil

2 pounds oxtails

½ onion, thinly sliced

2 celery stalks, chopped

1 carrot, chopped

¾ cup beef broth

1 tablespoon tomato paste

1 teaspoon kosher salt

1 teaspoon freshly ground black pepper

1 teaspoon garlic powder

1 teaspoon paprika

½ teaspoon ground ginger

1. Preheat the oven to 300°F.

2. In a nonstick frying pan, heat the oil over medium-high heat. Add the oxtails and brown them on all sides, 4 or 5 minutes. Transfer the oxtails to a baking dish and set aside.

3. Add the onion, celery, and carrot to the frying pan and cook over low heat, stirring frequently, for 5 minutes.

4. While the vegetables cook, prepare the oxtail by adding the beef broth, tomato paste, salt, pepper, garlic powder, paprika, and ginger to the baking dish with the oxtail.

5. Add the vegetables to the baking dish and stir until combined.

6. Cover the baking dish with aluminum foil and bake for 2 hours. Serve hot.

PER SERVING: FAT 59%; PROTEIN 37%; CARBS 4%; Calories: 813; Total fat: 53g; Protein: 75g; Total carbs: 9g; Fiber: 3g; Net carbs: 6g; Sodium: 1243mg; Iron: 8mg

Beef Casserole

PREP TIME: 15 minutes | **COOK TIME:** 3 hours | **SERVES 2**

This hearty beef casserole is my idea of the ultimate comfort food. It tastes better as the days go on, so go ahead and store the leftovers in the refrigerator and enjoy them the next day! The sauce is plentiful, so you can add any that is leftover to another dish. And trust me on the anchovy: it doesn't add fishiness but rather a depth of flavor to the sauce that is well worth it.

1 teaspoon kosher salt

1 teaspoon paprika

½ teaspoon freshly ground black pepper

1 pound top sirloin, 1 large piece or 2 pieces

2 tablespoons olive oil

5 cups beef broth, divided, plus ½ cup if needed

½ medium leek, trimmed, and thinly sliced

½ onion, thinly sliced

2 medium celery stalks, roughly chopped

1 small Anaheim pepper, seeded and roughly chopped

½ red bell pepper, seeded and roughly chopped

6 white mushrooms, trimmed and halved

1 anchovy, minced

1 tablespoon minced garlic

1 tablespoon soy sauce

1 tablespoon balsamic vinegar

1. Preheat the oven to 325°F.

2. In a small bowl, mix together the salt, paprika, and black pepper. Pat the meat dry with paper towels and rub the salt mixture on both sides of the meat.

3. In a Dutch oven, heat the olive oil over high heat. Add the steak and sear it for 3 minutes on each side. Transfer the steak to a plate and set aside. Turn off the heat.

4. Add ½ cup of beef broth to the Dutch oven and cook until it bubbles furiously. Deglaze the Dutch oven, using a spatula to scrape up any browned bits from the pan.

5. Reduce the heat to medium-high, add the leek, onion, celery, Anaheim pepper, bell pepper, mushrooms, anchovy, garlic, soy sauce, balsamic vinegar, Worcestershire sauce, and tomato paste, and stir until combined.

6. Add the remaining 4½ cups of beef broth and the bouillon powder and cook, gently stirring, until it begins to simmer.

7. Cover the Dutch oven, place it in the oven, and bake for 2 hours. Check the liquid to see if it is low. Add another ½ cup of broth if needed.

1 tablespoon Worcestershire
  sauce
2 tablespoons tomato paste
1 teaspoon beef
  bouillon powder

8. Bake for 1 hour more. Let the meat rest in the Dutch oven, covered, for 30 minutes before serving.

TIP: It is the long, slow cooking at a low temperature that tenderizes the meat. Don't be tempted to cook it on a higher heat for a shorter time. The meat will be tough.

PER SERVING: FAT %; PROTEIN %; CARBS %; Calories: 648; Total fat: 40g; Protein: 52g; Total carbs: 20g; Fiber: 4g; Net carbs: 16g; Sodium: 1,345mg; Iron: 6mg

Perfect Pork Chops

PREP TIME: 5 minutes | **COOK TIME:** 15 minutes | **SERVES 2**

An oven-safe, cast-iron pan lends itself perfectly to this recipe in which you start cooking on the stovetop and transfer the pan to the oven to complete the cooking. When you use this method, you will create a juicy and tender pork chop that melts in your mouth.

2 tablespoons olive oil

2 (11-ounce) bone-in pork chops

2 teaspoons kosher salt

2 teaspoons freshly ground black pepper

4 garlic cloves, peeled

½ small onion, thinly sliced

6 mushrooms, quartered (optional; see Tip)

1 sprig fresh rosemary

2 tablespoons salted butter

1. Preheat the oven to 400°F.

2. In a medium, cast-iron pan, heat the olive oil over high heat for 5 minutes.

3. Pat the pork chops dry with paper towels and season them on both sides with the salt and pepper.

4. Place the pork chops in the skillet and sear for 4 minutes without moving them. Add the garlic, onion, and mushrooms around the chops.

5. Turn the chops over, place the rosemary sprig on top, and add the butter to the skillet. Carefully place the skillet in the oven and roast for 8 minutes, or until the internal temperature of the pork chops reaches between 145°F and 155°F.

6. Remove from the oven, tent the skillet with aluminum foil, and let rest for 5 minutes before serving.

TIP: To make this a C4 dish, simply omit the mushrooms and onions.

PER SERVING: FAT 61%; PROTEIN 36%; CARBS 3%; Calories: 785; Total fat: 53g; Protein: 67g; Total carbs: 7g; Fiber: 2g; Net carbs: 5g; Sodium: 1431mg; Iron: 3mg

CK

Garlic and Herb Pork Loin Chop

PREP TIME: 10 minute | **COOK TIME:** 15 minutes | **SERVES 2**

This creamy pork recipe is a showstopper. Your guests will think that you have been cooking all day, but it actually comes together in under 30 minutes! The garlic and butter pair beautifully with the seasonings in this dish. You'll want to make this recipe all the time.

3 fresh basil leaves, chopped

4 garlic cloves, minced

1 tablespoon fresh thyme

5 tablespoons salted butter, melted

4 (3-ounce) boneless pork loin chops

1 teaspoon kosher salt

½ teaspoon freshly ground black pepper

1 teaspoon paprika

½ cup chicken broth

1 tablespoon freshly squeezed lemon juice

1 tablespoon heavy cream

1. In a small bowl, mix together the basil, garlic, thyme, and butter and set aside.

2. Pat the pork chops dry with paper towels and rub them all over with the salt, pepper, and paprika.

3. Heat a cast-iron pan over high heat for 3 minutes, or until it begins to smoke. Using tongs, place the pork chops in the skillet and cook for 3 minutes on each side. Transfer the pork chops to a plate and set aside.

4. Reduce the heat to low, pour in the chicken broth and lemon juice, and stir to deglaze the pan, scraping up any browned bits with a spatula, for about 1 minute. Add the cream and stir until combined.

5. Return the pork chops to the skillet and pour the herb and butter mixture into the pan. Reduce the heat to medium-low and cook for 5 minutes, using a spoon to baste the pork chops a couple of times.

6. Remove the pan from the heat, cover with aluminum foil, and let sit for 10 minutes. Serve immediately.

TIP: For best results, take the pork chops out of the refrigerator and let them sit for 30 minutes before cooking.

PER SERVING: FAT 69%; PROTEIN 29%; CARBS 2%; Calories: 561; Total fat: 44g; Protein: 38g; Total carbs: 4g; Fiber: 1g; Net carbs: 3g; Sodium: 896mg; Iron: 2mg

C4, CK

Lamb Kebabs

PREP TIME: 10 minutes plus overnight to marinate | **COOK TIME:** 10 minutes | **SERVES 2**

Lamb is highly nutritious and has great bioavailability. It is an excellent source of protein, fat, and especially iron. Marinating it overnight helps tenderize the meat and makes for a delicious meal. If you are using wooden skewers, make sure to soak them in water for at least 20 minutes before threading the lamb on them.

1 pound lamb leg steak, cut into 1-inch cubes
¼ cup avocado oil
½ teaspoon kosher salt
¼ teaspoon freshly ground black pepper
¼ teaspoon garlic powder
1 teaspoon Italian Spice Blend (page 126)

1. Place the lamb in a bowl or a zip-top plastic bag.

2. In a bowl, mix together the avocado oil, salt, pepper, garlic powder, and Italian spice blend to create the marinade. Pour the marinade over the lamb, seal the bag, and refrigerate it overnight.

3. Remove the lamb from the marinade and thread the chunks onto metal or wooden skewers.

4. Using a grill pan, cook the skewers, turning them once or twice, until the internal temperature reaches 145°F, about 10 minutes.

TIP: Pair this with Loaded Sour Cream (page 130).

PER SERVING: FAT 60%; PROTEIN 40%; CARBS 0%; Calories: 600; Total fat: 40g; Protein: 59g; Total carbs: 0g; Fiber: 0g; Net carbs: 0g; Sodium: 472mg; Iron: 5mg

Leg of Lamb

PREP TIME: 5 minutes | **COOK TIME:** 40 minutes | **SERVES 2**

Lamb is a fantastic source of quality protein. It is packed with vitamins and minerals, and regular consumption of lamb can actually promote muscle growth. This recipe is so juicy and delicious, even my lamb-skeptical children love it. It's perfect served straight from the oven, and just as delicious served cold the very next day.

1 teaspoon kosher salt

1 teaspoon garlic powder

1 teaspoon onion powder

2 (1-pound) lamb leg steaks

1 sprig fresh rosemary

1. Preheat the oven to 400°F.

2. In a small bowl, mix together the salt, garlic powder, and onion powder.

3. Pat the lamb dry with paper towels. Rub the salt mixture over both sides of the lamb steaks.

4. Heat a cast-iron pan over high heat until it begins to smoke. Reduce the heat to medium and sear the lamb steaks for 4 minutes per side. Place the rosemary sprig on top of the lamb.

5. Carefully transfer the hot skillet to the oven and roast for 30 minutes.

6. Remove from the oven and cover the lamb with aluminum foil. Let rest for 10 minutes.

TIP: Lamb is a lovely high-fat meat and will keep you satisfied longer than a leaner cut. For this reason, I recommend it in week 1 of the reset. Follow the recipe, but exclude the garlic powder, onion powder, and rosemary. Lamb is flavorful and the salt alone will be enough.

PER SERVING: FAT 63%; PROTEIN 37%; CARBS 0%;
Calories: 921; Total fat: 64g; Protein: 84g; Total carbs: 2g;
Fiber: 0g; Net carbs: 0g; Sodium: 847mg; Iron: 8mg

Whole Roast Chicken, 76

Poultry

C2, C3, C4, CK

Poached Chicken Breast

PREP TIME: 2 minutes | **COOK TIME:** 15 minutes | **SERVES 2**

Poaching chicken breasts is quick and easy, and the meat becomes moist and tender. You can add seasonings to the chicken, but in my opinion, it needs very little extra flavoring. This chicken is delicious hot or cold and can be used in a variety of dishes. Try it in the Chicken Lettuce Boats (page 82) or dice it up and add it to The Perfect Omelet (page 41) or the Meat Lover's Scramble (page 43). If you buy chicken breasts with the skin on, you can save the skins and use them to make the Crispy Chicken Skins (page 77).

2 (8-ounce) boneless, skinless chicken breasts

2 cups chicken broth

1. In a medium saucepan, combine the chicken and chicken broth and bring it to a boil over high heat.

2. Reduce the heat to medium and simmer for 15 minutes.

3. Remove the pan from the heat, cover, and let rest for 15 minutes.

4. Remove the chicken from the broth and, using two forks (or your hands), shred the meat.

TIP: To make this C1-appropriate, poach the chicken in water instead of chicken broth.

PER SERVING: FAT 20%; PROTEIN 80%; CARBS 0%; Calories: 272; Total fat: 6g; Protein: 50g; Total carbs: 0g; Fiber: 0g; Net carbs: 0g; Sodium: 102mg; Iron: 1mg

C3, C4, CK

Chicken Liver Pâté

PREP TIME: 5 minutes | **COOK TIME:** 20 minutes, plus 2 hours for chilling | **SERVES 8**

This recipe is a powerhouse of nutrition, rich with essential fatty acids and protein. It contains lots of iron, Vitamin B_{12}, and other vitamins and minerals. Serve it with Crispy Chicken Skins (page 77) or chopped vegetables.

2 cups cold water

2 teaspoons plus pinch kosher salt

2 eggs

5 tablespoons chicken fat, lard, or tallow

5 tablespoons salted butter

1 pound chicken livers

1 teaspoon freshly ground black pepper (optional)

1 teaspoon garlic powder (optional)

1 teaspoon onion powder (optional)

1. In a small saucepan, combine the water and a pinch of salt. Add the eggs and bring to a boil over medium-high heat. Remove the pan from the heat and let the eggs rest for 12 minutes. Peel the eggs under cold running water and set them aside.

2. In a large, nonstick frying pan, melt the chicken fat and butter over medium heat. Add the livers, pepper (if using), garlic powder (if using), and onion powder (if using); increase the heat to medium-high, and cook for 5 minutes. Turn the livers over using a firm, flat-ended spatula and cook for 5 minutes more.

3. Remove from the heat and let cool for 5 minutes.

4. Transfer the liver and any juices to a blender. Add the eggs to the blender and purée until smooth.

5. Divide the pâté equally among eight ramekins and let cool. Cover each ramekin with plastic wrap and refrigerate for at least 2 hours before serving.

TIP: Pour melted and cooled butter over the top of the pâté before refrigerating it to make it last up to 6 days.

PER SERVING: FAT 74%; PROTEIN 25%; CARBS 1%; Calories: 197; Total fat: 16g; Protein: 11g; Total carbs: 1g; Fiber: 0g; Net carbs: 1g; Sodium: 406mg; Iron: 5mg

Whole Roast Chicken

PREP TIME: 10 minutes | **COOK TIME:** 2 hours | **SERVES 4**

This simple-to-prepare, juicy chicken boasts delicate herb flavors that will have you reaching for seconds—but don't do it. Save it for a meal for the next day. That's a keto carnivore win!

1 (6-pound) whole chicken
½ onion, unpeeled
1 lemon, halved
2 sprigs fresh rosemary
2 sprigs fresh thyme
3 garlic cloves
¼ cup (½ stick) salted
  butter, cut into thin slices
¼ cup olive oil
½ tablespoon kosher salt
½ tablespoon freshly
  ground black pepper

1. Preheat the oven to 350°F.

2. Remove the neck and giblets from the cavity of the chicken and set them aside. Clean the bird and pat it dry with paper towels.

3. Place the chicken on a rack that fits into a roasting pan. Stuff the cavity of the chicken with the onion, lemon, rosemary, thyme, and garlic.

4. Using your fingers, gently pull back the chicken skin and slide the butter in the pocket it makes. Push the slices in as far as they will go.

5. Drizzle the outside of the chicken with the olive oil and season with the salt and pepper.

6. Roast for 2 hours, or until the temperature of the thickest part of the breast has reached 165°F. Tent the chicken with aluminum foil for 15 minutes before carving.

TIP: Store the bones, neck, and giblets from your chicken in the freezer and use them to make Chicken Bone Broth (page 128).

PER SERVING: FAT 70%; PROTEIN 30%; CARBS 0%; Calories: 1,117; Total fat: 87g; Protein: 77g; Total carbs: 1g; Fiber: 0g; Net carbs: 1g; Sodium: 818mg; Iron: 4mg

C4, CK

Crispy Chicken Skins

PREP TIME: 5 minutes | **COOK TIME:** 45 minutes | **SERVES 2**

Let's talk crispy chicken skins! In my humble opinion, these are even better than pork rinds. In addition to making a really great snack, you can slather them with chicken liver pâté, dip them into the Dill Dip (page 115), or serve them with any dish you would usually accompany with slices of bacon.

½ teaspoon kosher salt

½ teaspoon freshly ground black pepper

½ teaspoon smoked paprika

½ teaspoon garlic powder

Skin from 4 chicken breasts

1. Preheat the oven to 375°F. Line a baking sheet with parchment paper.

2. In a small bowl, mix together the salt, pepper, paprika, and garlic powder.

3. Place the skins on the baking sheet and sprinkle them with equal amounts of the spice mixture.

4. Cover the skins with another sheet of parchment paper and place a baking sheet on top to help weigh down the skins. Roast for 30 minutes or until crispy.

TIP: For a super-indulgent party snack, dip the skins in Loaded Sour Cream (page 130).

PER SERVING: FAT 82%; PROTEIN 16%; CARBS 2%; Calories: 282; Total fat: 26g; Protein: 10g; Total carbs: 1g; Fiber: 0g; Net carbs: 1g; Sodium: 341mg; Iron: 1mg

C4, CK

Luscious Lemon Chicken

PREP TIME: 10 minutes | **COOK TIME:** 10 minutes | **SERVES 2**

This dish, with its classic combination of butter, garlic, and lemon, comes together in 20 minutes and smells heavenly!

1 tablespoon Italian Spice Blend (page 126)

½ teaspoon kosher salt

½ teaspoon lemon pepper

⅓ cup grated Parmesan cheese

1 egg

2 (4-ounce) thin chicken breasts

2 tablespoons olive oil

¼ cup (½ stick) salted butter

1 garlic clove, minced

2 teaspoons freshly squeezed lemon juice

1. In a medium, shallow dish, combine the Italian spice blend, salt, lemon pepper, and Parmesan, and mix well.

2. In another shallow dish, whisk the egg.

3. Dip one chicken breast in the egg, making sure to completely cover it, and let any excess egg drip off. Place the chicken breast into the Parmesan mixture and press down gently. Turn the chicken over and press down again. Make sure the chicken is covered with the mixture on both sides. Set the coated chicken breast on a plate. Repeat with the other piece of chicken.

4. In a nonstick frying pan, heat the olive oil over medium-high heat for 2 minutes. Add the chicken and cook for 4 minutes. Turn the chicken and cook until the internal temperature reaches 165°F, about 4 minutes.

5. In a small, microwave-safe bowl, combine the butter, garlic, and lemon juice. Microwave for 15 seconds, or until the butter melts. Stir to combine.

6. Place the chicken on serving plates and pour the garlic butter equally over each piece of chicken.

PER SERVING: FAT 73%; PROTEIN 25%; CARBS 2%; Calories: 567; Total fat: 46g; Protein: 33g; Total carbs: 3g; Fiber: 0g; Net carbs: 3g; Sodium: 1,144mg; Iron: 1mg

Chicken Schnitzel

PREP TIME: 10 minutes | **COOK TIME:** 25 minutes | **SERVES 4**

Instead of breading and frying the chicken, which is the traditional method of making this dish, I've created a keto-friendly version that is quick and easy. Coating the meat with crushed pork rinds provides a crunchy crust.

Olive oil spray, for greasing
3 eggs
¾ cup crushed pork rinds
1 teaspoon kosher salt
½ teaspoon freshly ground
   black pepper
½ teaspoon paprika
   (optional)
4 (4-ounce) thin, boneless,
   skinless chicken breasts

1. Preheat the oven to 400°F. Line a baking sheet with parchment paper or a silicone mat. Grease the parchment or silicone mat with olive oil spray.

2. In a shallow bowl, whisk the eggs.

3. In a separate shallow bowl, mix together the pork rinds, salt, pepper, and paprika (if using).

4. Dip one chicken breast in the egg, making sure to completely cover it, and let any excess egg drip off. Place the chicken breast into the pork rind mixture and press down gently. Flip and press down again. Make sure the chicken is covered with the mixture on both sides. Place the chicken on the prepared baking sheet. Repeat with the rest of the chicken.

5. Spritz the surface of the schnitzel with a little olive oil spray, as this will help it crisp up in the oven.

6. Bake for 25 to 28 minutes, or until the internal temperature has reached 165°F. Serve hot.

PER SERVING: FAT 38%; PROTEIN 62%; CARBS 0%; Calories: 234; Total fat: 10g; Protein: 36g; Total carbs: 0g; Fiber: 0g; Net carbs: 0g; Sodium: 463mg; Iron: 1mg

C4, CK

Chicken Stroganoff

PREP TIME: 5 minutes | **COOK TIME:** 20 minutes | **SERVES 4**

With its origins in 19th-century Russia, stroganoff is traditionally made with beef and sour cream and served over noodles or rice. For my version, I've used chicken tenders and replaced the sour cream with heavy cream because I think it gives a wonderful depth of flavor. This is savory and creamy, while fitting nicely into a keto diet. It tastes amazing on its own, though you could spoon it over Cauliflower Rice (page 117) if you wanted something a little heartier.

¼ cup (½ stick) salted butter

1 tablespoon olive oil

1½ pound chicken tenders, each cut into 3 pieces

½ small onion, sliced

3 garlic cloves, minced

6 ounces white mushrooms, stemmed and quartered

½ cup chicken broth

2 tablespoons balsamic vinegar

½ tablespoon Dijon mustard

1 teaspoon kosher salt

1 teaspoon freshly ground black pepper

½ cup heavy cream

1. In a large, nonstick frying pan, heat the butter and olive oil over high heat. Add the chicken and brown it on all sides, about 4 minutes per side. Transfer the chicken to a plate and set aside.

2. Reduce the heat to medium-low, combine the onions and garlic in the pan, and cook for 3 minutes. Add the mushrooms, broth, balsamic vinegar, Dijon mustard, salt, and pepper, and gently stir until combined.

3. Add the cream, return the chicken to the pan, and stir until the chicken is covered in the sauce.

4. Increase the heat to medium and simmer, stirring occasionally, until the chicken is cooked through, about 12 minutes. Serve immediately.

PER SERVING: FAT 56%; PROTEIN 22%; CARBS 22%; Calories: 654; Total fat: 40g; Protein: 36g; Total carbs: 36g; Fiber: 1g; Net carbs: 35g; Sodium: 1,557mg; Iron: 3mg

CK

Lemon and Mustard Marinated Chicken

PREP TIME: 10 minutes plus 4 hours to overnight to marinate | **COOK TIME:** 15 minutes | **SERVES 2**

Marinating the chicken gives it incredibly deep flavor and a succulent texture. Also, the longer it marinates, the juicier it becomes. Serve it with a simple side dish of steamed broccoli as a quick weeknight meal or place slices of the chicken over greens for a filling lunch.

½ cup full-fat Greek yogurt

1 tablespoon freshly squeezed lemon juice

1 tablespoon Dijon mustard

1 teaspoon kosher salt

½ teaspoon freshly ground black pepper

2 (6-ounce) boneless, skinless chicken breasts

1 tablespoon olive oil

2 tablespoons salted butter

1. In a small bowl, mix together the yogurt, lemon juice, Dijon mustard, salt, and pepper.

2. Place the chicken in a wide, shallow bowl. Pour the yogurt mixture over the chicken, making sure the chicken is submerged. Cover the bowl with plastic wrap and refrigerate it for at least 4 hours or overnight.

3. In a nonstick frying pan, heat the olive oil over medium-high heat for 2 minutes. Shake any excess marinade off the chicken, place each breast in the frying pan, cover, and cook for 5 minutes. Turn the chicken over, cover, and cook until it reaches an internal temperature of 165°F, about 5 minutes more.

4. Transfer the chicken to a cutting board and cut it into slices.

5. Melt the butter in the frying pan. Return the chicken to the pan, and cook, stirring constantly to coat it in the melted butter, for about 2 minutes.

TIP: Add some heat by including ¼ teaspoon of your favorite hot sauce along with the butter.

PER SERVING: FAT 54%; PROTEIN 42%; CARBS 4%; Calories: 411; Total fat: 25g; Protein: 41g; Total carbs: 4g; Fiber: 1g; Net carbs: 3g; Sodium: 573mg; Iron: 1mg

Chicken Lettuce Boats

PREP TIME: 10 minutes | **COOK TIME:** 30 minutes | **SERVES 2**

Chicken salad is always a popular choice and is simple to make. Having a lettuce wrap is such a great alternative to a traditional bread-based sandwich. The chicken salad is scooped onto the lettuce leaves, which serve as the "boat." Eat it with a knife and fork or wrap up the lettuce and eat it with your hands.

1 pound boneless skinless chicken breast

2 cups water

⅓ cup avocado oil mayonnaise

2 tablespoons sour cream

1 tablespoon freshly squeezed lemon juice

1 teaspoon mustard powder

½ tablespoon fresh parsley, finely chopped

1 teaspoon fresh dill, finely chopped

2 scallions, finely chopped

2 celery stalks, finely chopped

¼ cup walnut pieces

½ teaspoon kosher salt

½ teaspoon freshly ground black pepper

2 large romaine lettuce leaves

1. In a medium saucepan, combine the chicken and water and bring it to a boil over high heat. Reduce the heat to medium and simmer for 15 minutes.

2. Remove the pan from the heat, cover, and let rest for 15 minutes.

3. Remove the chicken from the pan, place it in a bowl, cover with plastic wrap, and let cool in the refrigerator.

4. In a small bowl, mix together the mayonnaise, sour cream, lemon juice, and mustard powder. Add the parsley, dill, scallions, celery, walnuts, salt, and pepper, and stir until combined.

5. Cut up the cooled chicken into small pieces, add it to the salad, and stir until combined.

6. Using a large ice cream scoop or a serving spoon, divide the chicken salad equally between the two lettuce leaves.

TIP: Try adding a handful of blueberries if you prefer your salad to have a little sweetness. Just remember to account for them in your macros.

PER SERVING: FAT 60%; PROTEIN 35%; CARBS 5%; Calories: 674; Total fat: 46g; Protein: 55g; Total carbs: 10g; Fiber: 3g; Net carbs: 7g; Sodium: 656mg; Iron: 2mg

CK

Chicken Curry

PREP TIME: 5 minutes | **COOK TIME:** 45 minutes | **SERVES 4**

When it comes to simplicity, this dish wins hands down. The oven does most of the hard work. The blend of the rich, aromatic spices brings a deeply comforting flavor to this dish. It is rich, creamy, and one of my favorite recipes in the book. Serve it over Cauliflower Rice (page 117).

1½ pounds chicken tenders

¾ cup sour cream

1 tablespoon garam masala

1 teaspoon ground cinnamon

1 teaspoon ground ginger

1 teaspoon kosher salt

½ teaspoon freshly ground black pepper

½ teaspoon paprika

¼ teaspoon cayenne pepper

4 tablespoons tomato paste

3 garlic cloves, minced

1 tablespoon dried minced onion

2 tablespoons olive oil

1. Preheat the oven to 375°F.

2. Place the chicken tenders into a medium baking dish with a lid.

3. In a medium bowl, mix together the sour cream, garam masala, cinnamon, ginger, salt, black pepper, paprika, cayenne pepper, tomato paste, garlic, dried onion, and olive oil.

4. Pour the sauce over the chicken, making sure that all the tenders are coated with the mixture.

5. Cover and bake for 45 minutes, or until the sauce is bubbling. Serve warm.

TIP: To add more heat, add another ½ teaspoon of cayenne pepper.

PER SERVING: FAT 48%; PROTEIN 46%; CARBS 6%; Calories: 351; Total fat: 18g; Protein: 40g; Total carbs: 7g; Fiber: 1g; Net carbs: 6g; Sodium: 408mg; Iron: 2mg

Chicken Noodle Soup

PREP TIME: 15 minutes | **COOK TIME:** 2 hours, 15 minutes | **SERVES 2**

I have been making chicken soup as long as I have had my own kitchen. It's one of those soups that's incredibly nutritious and is what everyone wants to eat when they need something warm, filling, and comforting.

7 cups chicken
broth, divided

1 cup water

1 large tomato

½ onion

2 carrots, peeled and each
cut into 4 pieces

2 celery stalks, trimmed

2 tablespoons chicken
bouillon powder

2 teaspoons kosher salt

1 teaspoon freshly ground
black pepper

3½ ounces shirataki
noodles

2 teaspoons chopped fresh
parsley

Poached Chicken Breast
(page 74)

1. In a large stockpot, combine 6 cups of chicken broth and the water, cover, and bring to a boil over high heat.

2. Reduce the heat to medium and add the whole tomato, onion, carrot, celery, chicken bouillon powder, salt, and pepper, and stir until combined.

3. Reduce the heat to low and simmer for 2 hours.

4. Prepare the noodles 10 minutes before the soup is ready. Hold the noodles under cold water for 2 minutes. In a small saucepan, bring the remaining 1 cup of chicken broth to a boil over high heat. Add the noodles, parsley, and chicken and cook for 2 minutes.

5. Using a slotted spoon, discard the onion, celery, and tomato. Add the chicken, noodles, and broth to the stockpot and stir to combine.

6. Spoon into bowls and serve.

TIP: If you have soup left over, store it in an airtight container and refrigerate it for up to 3 days or freeze it for up to 3 months.

PER SERVING (1 BOWL OF SOUP): FAT 12%; PROTEIN 69%; CARBS 19%; Calories: 300; Total fat: 4g; Protein: 52g; Total carbs: 14g; Fiber: 4g; Net carbs: 10g; Sodium: 1,419mg; Iron: 3mg

Turkey Burger

PREP TIME: 5 minutes | **COOK TIME:** 10 minutes | **SERVES 2**

Turkey burgers are a wonderful alternative to traditional beef. With this recipe, your burger will come out juicy and delicious. Top it with your favorite cheese, whether its Cheddar, American, or even blue cheese. A few slices of tomato and avocado plus a side salad round out the meal. Look for 85% lean and 15% fat ground turkey for the best flavor.

1 pound 85/15 ground turkey

2 tablespoons grated Parmesan cheese

2 teaspoons Worcestershire sauce

½ teaspoon garlic powder

½ teaspoon onion powder

1 tablespoon finely chopped fresh parsley

½ teaspoon kosher salt

Pinch freshly ground black pepper

2 tablespoons avocado oil

1. In a bowl, mix together the ground turkey, Parmesan, Worcestershire sauce, garlic powder, onion powder, parsley, salt, and pepper until fully combined. Form two patties of equal size, about ½-inch thick.

2. In a medium, nonstick frying pan, heat the oil over medium-high heat for 2 minutes.

3. Place the patties in the pan and cook for 5 minutes. Carefully flip over the patties and cook until the internal temperature reaches 165°F, 4 or 5 minutes more.

TIP: Do not press the burgers flat into the pan with your spatula as they cook, as this will release juices that you want to keep in the burger.

PER SERVING: FAT 60%; PROTEIN 38%; CARBS 2%; Calories: 490; Total fat: 33g; Protein: 46g; Total carbs: 3g; Fiber: 0g; Net carbs: 3g; Sodium: 571mg; Iron: 3mg

Turkey Meatza

PREP TIME: 15 minutes | **COOK TIME:** 30 minutes | **SERVES 3**

Eating a carb-restricted diet means that regular pizza dough is not on the menu. But you can still have pizza! With an ingenious mixture of almond flour, cream cheese, eggs, and—yes—turkey, this new-fangled crust is super low-carb and a great base for marinara and mozzarella.

¼ cup cream cheese, at room temperature

¼ cup egg whites

¼ cup almond flour

½ teaspoon xanthan gum

3 teaspoons kosher salt, divided

1 teaspoon freshly ground black pepper, divided

2 tablespoons Italian Spice Blend (page 126)

2 pounds lean ground turkey

¾ cup marinara sauce

1 teaspoon garlic salt

¼ cup grated Parmesan cheese

¼ cup chopped fresh basil

1 cup grated mozzarella cheese

1. Preheat the oven to 350°F. Line a 12-by-17-inch rimmed baking sheet with parchment paper big enough to overlap the edges on all sides by about 2 inches.

2. In a large bowl, mix together the cream cheese and egg whites with a large spoon until they are fully combined and the cheese has softened.

3. Add the almond flour, xanthan gum, 2 teaspoons of the salt, ½ teaspoon of the pepper, and the Italian spice blend and stir until combined.

4. Add the turkey and mix with a large spoon until combined.

5. Place the mixture onto the parchment-lined baking sheet and gently press it into the pan all the way to the edges. Use your thumb to create a thicker crust around the edges by pushing a little extra turkey mixture along the edge of the pan.

6. Bake for 20 minutes. Remove the pan from the oven and carefully pour off any excess liquid that has accumulated and blot the base with a paper towel. The base shrinks a little when it bakes, so gently flatten out the crust so it will fill the pan all the way to the edges.

7. Increase the oven temperature to 400°F.

8. Slide the pizza crust along with the parchment paper onto a large baking sheet by holding onto the parchment and lifting it carefully out of the pan.

9. Pour the marinara sauce over the base and spread it out evenly, leaving the crust bare around the edges. Sprinkle the garlic salt, the remaining ½ teaspoon of pepper, the Parmesan, and the basil over the entire crust. Sprinkle the mozzarella and the remaining 1 teaspoon of kosher salt over the top.

10. Bake for 8 minutes. Turn the oven to broil and bake for 2 minutes more, or until the crust is browned and the cheese is melted.

11. Cut the meatza into six pieces and serve.

TIP: Use a marinara sauce that has no more than a total of 3 grams of carbs per ¼ cup.

PER SERVING: FAT 57%; PROTEIN 39%; CARBS 4%; Calories: 741; Total fat: 47g; Protein: 73g; Total carbs: 8g; Fiber: 2g; Net carbs: 6g; Sodium: 1,867mg; Iron: 5mg

Smoky Turkey Cutlets

PREP TIME: 2 minutes | **COOK TIME:** 10 minutes | **SERVES 2**

Some people find turkey bland, though in this recipe it's packed with the pungent flavors from my Smoky Spice Blend, which is loaded with smoked paprika, cayenne pepper, garlic, and onion. If you have the blend ready ahead of time, you can have dinner on the table in 10 minutes. And my secret to keeping the cutlets moist? Cook the turkey with the lid on the frying pan, which will keep in those lovely juices.

2 (½-pound) turkey breast cutlets

1 tablespoon Smoky Spice Blend (page 124)

2 tablespoons olive oil

1. Pat the turkey dry with paper towels and rub the smoky spice blend equally all over the cutlets.

2. In a large, nonstick frying pan, heat the olive oil over medium-high heat until the oil starts to smoke.

3. Reduce the heat to medium. Add the cutlets, cover, and cook for 3 minutes. Turn over the cutlets, cover, and cook until the internal temperature reaches 165°F, about 3 minutes more.

TIP: Pair this recipe with Dill Dip (page 115).

PER SERVING: FAT 58%; PROTEIN 42%; CARBS 0%; Calories: 373; Total fat: 18g; Protein: 51g; Total carbs: 0g; Fiber: 0g; Net carbs: 0g; Sodium: 268mg; Iron: 2mg

Sizzling Salmon, page 93

Fish and Seafood

C2, C3, C4, CK

Seared Scallops

PREP TIME: 5 minutes | **COOK TIME:** 5 minutes | **SERVES 2**

Scallops require very few embellishments to taste absolutely wonderful, and for this recipe, all you need is a little salt, black pepper, garlic, and oil for the pan. The key to cooking them is to use a cast-iron pan, which will get hot enough to give the scallops a gorgeous sear with a mouthwatering caramelization that you will love. And this meal goes from the stove to the dinner table in less than 10 minutes. How great is that?

1 pound scallops

½ teaspoon kosher salt

½ teaspoon freshly ground
   black pepper

2 tablespoons avocado oil

3 tablespoons salted butter

1 tablespoon dried
   minced garlic

1. Pat the scallops dry with paper towels and season them all over with the salt and pepper.

2. In a cast-iron pan, heat the avocado oil over medium-high heat until it begins to smoke. Add the scallops and cook for 2 minutes.

3. Turn over each scallop and add the butter and garlic to the skillet. Cook for 2 minutes more.

4. Remove from the heat and serve warm.

TIP: Pair this recipe with Lemon and Garlic Asparagus (page 116).

PER SERVING: FAT 66%; PROTEIN 24%; CARBS 10%; Calories: 441; Total fat: 32g; Protein: 28g; Total carbs: 9g; Fiber: 0g; Net carbs: 9g; Sodium: 1,318mg; Iron: 1mg

C4, CK

Sizzling Salmon

PREP TIME: 5 minutes | **COOK TIME:** 10 minutes | **SERVES 2**

Salmon is an excellent choice if you are eating clean keto or on a strict carnivore diet because it is loaded with protein and rich in vitamins, minerals, and antioxidants. This is another recipe that will make great use of a cast-iron pan, which excels at developing wonderful caramelization and searing.

2 (5-ounce) salmon
 steaks, skin on
2 teaspoons kosher salt
½ teaspoon freshly ground
 black pepper
2 teaspoons salted butter

1. Remove the salmon from the refrigerator and let it sit at room temperature for 10 minutes before cooking.

2. Heat a cast-iron pan over medium-high heat until it begins to smoke, about 4 minutes.

3. Season the salmon on both sides with the salt and pepper. Place the salmon in the skillet and cook, skin-side up, over medium heat for 4 minutes.

4. Turn the salmon over and cook until it reaches a temperature of 145°F, about 5 minutes. If your salmon is very thick, it may need a minute more.

5. Transfer the salmon to plates, top each steak with 1 teaspoon of butter, and serve warm.

TIP: To make this recipe C3-appropriate, omit the butter and black pepper.

PER SERVING: FAT 51%; PROTEIN 48%; CARBS 1%; Calories: 235; Total fat: 13g; Protein: 28g; Total carbs: 0g; Fiber: 0g; Net carbs: 0g; Sodium: 1,256mg; Iron: 1mg

C4, CK

Blackened Cod

PREP TIME: 5 minutes | **COOK TIME:** 10 minutes | **SERVES 2**

Cod is a lovely meaty fish that is quite versatile because its mild flavor adapts to a wide range of spices. The blend of seasonings in this recipe includes paprika, oregano, thyme, and just a bit of ground ginger, which gives the cod an intriguing extra level of complexity. Serve it with a green salad or some steamed or roasted vegetables.

4 teaspoons paprika
1 teaspoon ground oregano
1 teaspoon ground thyme
1 teaspoon garlic powder
1 teaspoon cayenne pepper
½ teaspoon ground ginger
2 (½-pound) cod loin fillets
4 tablespoons avocado oil, divided

1. In a wide, shallow dish, combine the paprika, oregano, thyme, garlic powder, cayenne pepper, and ginger. Set aside.

2. Pat the fish dry with paper towels and drizzle 2 tablespoons of avocado oil all over both pieces. Dip each piece of cod into the dry seasoning mix and press down firmly to coat all sides of the fish equally.

3. In a large, cast-iron pan, heat the remaining 2 tablespoons of avocado oil over high heat until it begins to smoke, about 2 minutes.

4. Reduce the heat to medium-high, place both pieces of fish into the skillet, and cook for 4 minutes. Using a wide spatula, carefully turn the fish over (it will be delicate at this point) and cook for 4 minutes more.

5. Transfer the cod to plates and serve warm.

TIP: This recipe works very well with boneless skinless salmon, too.

PER SERVING: FAT 61%; PROTEIN 35%; CARBS 4%; Calories: 428; Total fat: 30g; Protein: 36g; Total carbs: 5g; Fiber: 2g; Net carbs: 3g; Sodium: 692mg; Iron: 2mg

C4, CK

Fried Cod with Parmesan Crust

PREP TIME: 10 minutes | **COOK TIME:** 8 minutes | **SERVES 2**

Like so many other people, I grew up with fish sticks. Now that I'm an adult, I still want that comforting crunchy treat, but when eating keto carnivore I need to avoid the preservatives. So, I created this more mature version and it's absolutely delicious. One thing that I like about eating carnivore is that fried food is totally acceptable.

1 cup avocado oil

½ cup grated
   Parmesan cheese

1 tablespoon dried
   minced onion

½ teaspoon paprika

1 teaspoon kosher salt

½ teaspoon freshly ground
   black pepper

1 egg, whisked

1 pound cod loin fillet, cut
   into 8 pieces

1. Fill a large, nonstick frying pan with 1 inch of avocado oil and heat it over medium-high heat to 350°F. Use your meat thermometer to check the oil temperature. You may not need all the oil.

2. In a shallow dish, mix together the Parmesan, dried onion, paprika, salt, and pepper.

3. Place the egg in another shallow dish.

4. Dip each piece of fish into the egg, let any excess drip off, and then dip the fish into the Parmesan mixture.

5. Place the fish in the pan and fry for 4 or 5 minutes. Using a spatula, carefully turn the fish over and fry it until it is crispy and golden, 4 or 5 minutes more.

PER SERVING: **FAT 51%; PROTEIN 45%; CARBS 4%;** Calories: 426; Total fat: 24g; Protein: 45g; Total carbs: 5g; Fiber: 0g; Net carbs: 5g; Sodium: 1,756mg; Iron: 1mg

Panfried Tilapia with Garlic and Lemon

PREP TIME: 5 minutes | **COOK TIME:** 10 minutes | **SERVES 2**

Tilapia is another lovely white-fleshed fish with a mild flavor. You can season it with a lot of different ingredients and it can be used instead of other fish like cod when availability is an issue. Lemon and garlic is one of my favorite combinations and it really sings here. Serve this fish with some roasted broccoli or Lemon and Garlic Asparagus (page 116).

2 tablespoons grated
  Parmesan cheese
½ teaspoon kosher salt
¼ teaspoon freshly ground
  black pepper
2 (½-pound) boneless
  skinless tilapia fillets
2 tablespoons olive oil
4 tablespoons salted
  butter, divided
Zest and juice of ½ lemon
1 garlic clove, minced
1 tablespoon chopped
  fresh parsley

1. In a small bowl, combine the Parmesan, salt, and pepper, and mix well. Set aside.

2. Pat the fish dry with paper towels and drizzle the olive oil equally on both sides. Rub the fish with the Parmesan mixture.

3. In a nonstick frying pan, melt 2 tablespoons of the butter over medium-high heat until it bubbles. Add the fish and cook for 4 minutes. Using a spatula, carefully turn the fish over and cook it until it's crispy and golden, about 4 minutes more.

4. Transfer the fish to plates and set aside.

5. Reduce the heat to medium, combine the remaining 2 tablespoons of butter, the lemon zest and juice, garlic, and parsley and cook for 2 minutes. Pour the butter sauce over the fish and serve.

TIP: Add some chopped fresh dill or rosemary to the Parmesan mixture for some extra zest.

PER SERVING: FAT 66%; PROTEIN 33%; CARBS 1%; Calories: 568; Total fat: 41g; Protein: 47g; Total carbs: 2g; Fiber: 0g; Net carbs: 2g; Sodium: 683mg; Iron: 2mg

C4, CK

Garlic Shrimp

PREP TIME: 5 minutes | **COOK TIME:** 10 minutes | **SERVES 2**

Using minced fresh garlic and freshly squeezed lemon juice gives this shrimp a one-two punch of flavor, so don't be tempted to use dried garlic or lemon juice from a bottle. Shrimp cooks extremely quicky, so pay attention to the cook time and be ready to remove them from the pan at the right moment. Serve these with a green vegetable or Mozzarella Bites (page 114).

1 pound large shrimp, deveined, tails on
½ teaspoon kosher salt
½ teaspoon lemon pepper
3 tablespoons salted butter
2 garlic cloves, minced
½ small lemon

1. Pat the shrimp dry with paper towels and season them with the salt and lemon pepper.

2. In a large, nonstick frying pan, melt the butter over medium-high heat until it begins to sizzle.

3. Add the garlic and shrimp and cook for 3 minutes. Turn the shrimp over and cook until they turn opaque, about 3 minutes more.

4. Divide the shrimp equally between two plates and squeeze the lemon on top. Serve immediately.

TIP: For a stricter version of this dish, simply omit the garlic and lemon. The buttery salt and lemon pepper flavor is still delicious.

PER SERVING: FAT 46%; PROTEIN 52%; CARBS 2%; Calories: 353; Total fat: 18g; Protein: 46g; Total carbs: 2g; Fiber: 0g; Net carbs: 2g; Sodium: 698mg; Iron: 1mg

C4, CK

Citrus-Ginger Crab Cakes

PREP TIME: 15 minutes, plus 10 minutes to refrigerate | **COOK TIME:** 20 minutes | **MAKES 9 CRAB CAKES**

I absolutely love all the savory flavors that come together in these crab cakes, and the soy sauce, lemon, and lime give this meal a southeast Asian feel. It's my favorite recipe in the book!

½ cup avocado oil

½ cup (1 stick) salted butter

1 egg

¼ cup sour cream

2 tablespoons avocado oil mayonnaise

1 tablespoon freshly squeezed lemon juice

1 tablespoon soy sauce

1 teaspoon ground ginger

1 teaspoon kosher salt

½ teaspoon freshly ground black pepper

½ teaspoon garlic powder

½ teaspoon paprika

1 scallion, finely chopped

1 tablespoon finely chopped fresh parsley

1 teaspoon lime zest

1 teaspoon lemongrass paste (optional)

1 pound lump crabmeat

½ cup grated Parmesan cheese

1. In a large, nonstick frying pan, heat the avocado oil and butter over low heat.

2. In a large bowl, whisk together the egg, sour cream, mayonnaise, lemon juice, soy sauce, ginger, salt, pepper, garlic powder, and paprika.

3. Add the scallion, parsley, lime zest, and lemongrass (if using) and mix until combined. Add the crab and Parmesan and mix until combined.

4. Using a ¼ cup as a measure, form nine crab patties and place them on a plate. Cover them with plastic wrap and refrigerate for 10 minutes. They will be wet but they should still hold together.

5. Cooking in two batches to avoid overcrowding the pan, add four of the crab patties to the pan. Increase the heat to medium and cook for 4 minutes. Use a spatula to flatten the crab cakes slightly.

6. Turn the crab cakes over and cook them until they are golden brown and reach an internal temperature of 165°F, about 4 minutes more. Transfer the crab cakes to a plate and repeat from step 6 with the remaining five crab patties.

PER SERVING (3 CRAB CAKES): FAT 58%; PROTEIN 34%; CARBS 8%;
Calories: 432; Total fat: 28g; Protein: 34g; Total carbs: 9g;
Fiber: 1g; Net carbs: 8g; Sodium: 1,298mg; Iron: 1mg

C4, CK

Salmon Fritters

PREP TIME: 15 minutes | **COOK TIME:** 10 minutes | **SERVES 2**

When I was young, I was not a fan of seafood, so my mama made these for me and it was the only way she could get me to eat fish. I have adjusted her recipe a little to suit my grown-up taste buds and keto requirements, including using my Seafood Spice Blend, which is a mix of dill, onion powder, parsley, garlic, and lemon pepper. Salmon is well known for its wealth of omega-3 fatty acids and is rich in protein and vitamin D as well.

¾ cup avocado oil

3 (5-ounce) cans salmon

1 egg, whisked

2 teaspoons Seafood Spice Blend (page 125)

1 tablespoon freshly squeezed lemon juice

¼ cup avocado oil mayonnaise

1 tablespoon low-sugar ketchup

½ teaspoon yellow mustard

1 tablespoon Parmesan cheese

1 tablespoon almond flour

1. In a large, nonstick frying pan, heat the avocado oil over medium heat until it reaches between 350°F and 375°F.

2. In a large bowl, combine the salmon, egg, seafood spice blend, lemon juice, mayonnaise, ketchup, mustard, Parmesan, and almond flour and mix well with an electric hand mixer or a sturdy spoon.

3. Using a ¼-cup measure, form the mixture into six patties and, using your hands, flatten each one.

4. Add the patties to the pan and fry for 3 minutes. Using a spatula, gently turn the patties over and fry them until they're crispy and browned, about 3 minutes more.

5. Transfer the fritters to plates and serve warm.

TIP: Pay attention to the smoke point of oils, which is the temperature at which it burns. Olive oil has a low smoke point so it is fine for sautéing but not so good for high-temperature cooking methods like frying. Avocado oil has one of the highest smoke points and I use it whenever I fry.

PER SERVING (3 PATTIES): FAT 71%; PROTEIN 28%; CARBS 1%;
Calories: 707; Total fat: 56g; Protein: 50g; Total carbs: 2g;
Fiber: 0g; Net carbs: 2g; Sodium: 926mg; Iron: 1mg

Tuna Salad

PREP TIME: 10 minutes | **SERVES 4**

This is truly the best tuna salad I've ever tasted, if I do say so myself. Dill is one of my favorite herbs, and mixed with the other ingredients, it gives this dish a distinctive, fresh, lemony flavor. I prefer to use dried dill instead of fresh in this particular recipe because it is less bitter. Enjoy this tuna for a light lunch with a chopped green salad.

3 (5-ounce) cans tuna packed in olive oil, drained

½ cup avocado or other keto-friendly mayonnaise

¼ cup sour cream

2 celery stalks, finely chopped

2 scallions, finely chopped

¼ teaspoon kosher salt

¼ teaspoon freshly ground black pepper

1 kosher dill pickle spear, finely chopped

½ teaspoon dried dill

2 teaspoons Worcestershire sauce

1. In a medium bowl, flake the tuna with a fork as finely as you can.

2. Add the mayonnaise, sour cream, celery, scallions, salt, pepper, dill pickle, dill, and Worcestershire sauce and mix until well combined.

3. Store leftovers in an airtight container in the refrigerator for up to 1 week.

TIP: To make this a more traditional keto recipe, add 1 tablespoon of pumpkin seeds to the mixture.

PER SERVING: FAT 72%; PROTEIN 26%; CARBS 2%; Calories: 381; Total fat: 30g; Protein: 23g; Total carbs: 2g; Fiber: 1g; Net carbs: 1g; Sodium: 703mg; Iron: 1mg

C4, CK

Shrimp Salad

PREP TIME: 10 minutes | **COOK TIME:** 4 minutes | **SERVES 4**

For this recipe, to create a twist on the classic shrimp salad, I turned to grapefruit zest and a little grapefruit juice. They give this dish a really nice tang and delicious flavor. Shrimp is high in protein, vitamins, and minerals, so it's a great choice when eating clean keto or carnivore. I use avocado oil instead of olive oil because it has a milder flavor that doesn't interfere with the other ingredients. Eat the shrimp on its own or add it to a lovely green salad for a light yet filling meal.

2 tablespoons avocado oil

1 pound shelled and
   deveined shrimp

½ cup avocado oil
   mayonnaise

1 tablespoon grapefruit zest

1 tablespoon freshly
   squeezed grapefruit juice

½ teaspoon ground ginger

½ teaspoon kosher salt

½ teaspoon freshly ground
   black pepper

¼ teaspoon paprika

1. In a large, nonstick frying pan, heat the avocado oil over medium heat for about 2 minutes. Place half of the shrimp into the pan and cook until the bottoms are seared, 2 or 3 minutes.

2. Turn each shrimp over and cook until the shrimp are seared, opaque, and cooked through, about 2 minutes more. Transfer the shrimp to a plate.

3. Repeat with the remaining shrimp and transfer them to the plate. Let cool.

4. To make the dressing, in a large bowl, mix together the mayonnaise, grapefruit zest, grapefruit juice, ginger, salt, pepper, and paprika.

5. Once the shrimp have cooled completely, add them to the dressing and mix until combined, making sure the shrimp are evenly coated.

6. Serve immediately.

TIP: For a stricter carnivore diet, use lemon juice instead of grapefruit juice to lower the sugar.

PER SERVING: FAT 72%; PROTEIN 27%; CARBS 1%; Calories: 349; Total fat: 28g; Protein: 23g; Total carbs: 1g; Fiber: 0g; Net carbs: 1g; Sodium: 455mg; Iron: 1mg

CK

Cod Sofrito

PREP TIME: 15 minutes | **COOK TIME:** 25 minutes | **SERVES 2**

Sofrito is a versatile sauce made from tomatoes, peppers, onion, and garlic. There are many variations of this sauce, and my own is inspired by my love of Mediterranean flavors and cooking. You can make the sauce on its own without the cod and add it to almost any protein dish.

2 tablespoons olive oil

½ medium onion,
  finely chopped

2 (8-ounce) boneless
  skinless cod loin fillets

1 teaspoon kosher salt

1 teaspoon freshly ground
  black pepper

1 teaspoon paprika

3 garlic cloves, minced

1 scallion, finely chopped

3 large tomatoes

½ Anaheim pepper, seeded
  and chopped

½ red bell pepper, seeded
  and chopped

2 tablespoons tomato paste

½ teaspoon ground oregano

½ teaspoon ground thyme

½ cup chicken broth

1. Preheat the oven to 350°F.

2. In a Dutch oven, heat the olive oil over medium heat. Add the onions and sauté for 10 minutes.

3. Rub the fish with the salt, black pepper, and paprika on both sides and place it on a plate. Set aside.

4. To the Dutch oven, add the garlic, scallion, tomatoes, Anaheim pepper, bell pepper, tomato paste, oregano, thyme, and chicken broth, and cook, stirring frequently, until it simmers. Remove from the heat, add the fish to the pan, and cover it with the sauce.

5. Cover and bake for 25 minutes. Remove from the heat. Let rest, covered, for 15 minutes.

6. Spoon onto plates and serve immediately.

TIP: Store any leftover sauce in an airtight container in the refrigerator for up to 5 days.

PER SERVING: FAT 36%; PROTEIN 43%; CARBS 21%; Calories: 374; Total fat: 15g; Protein: 39g; Total carbs: 22g; Fiber: 6g; Net carbs: 16g; Sodium: 1,511mg; Iron: 3mg

CK

Baked Halibut

PREP TIME: 5 minutes | **COOK TIME:** 15 minutes | **SERVES 2**

Halibut is not only a wonderful source of protein but is also full of great nutrients and vitamins, particularly omega-3 fatty acids and magnesium. With a firm texture and mild flavor, it's a great place to start if you are not a regular fish eater. I think you'll really like the crispy topping and the punchy flavor thanks to the Worcestershire sauce and spicy brown mustard. All you need is a simple salad of greens, and dinner is good to go.

Olive oil spray, for greasing

2 (6-ounce) boneless
  skinless halibut fillets

¼ cup grated
  Parmesan cheese

2 tablespoons almond flour

1 tablespoon spicy
  brown mustard

1 tablespoon Worcestershire
  sauce

½ teaspoon kosher salt

1. Preheat the oven to 400°F. Line a rimmed baking sheet with aluminum foil and grease the foil with olive oil spray.

2. Place both pieces of fish on the prepared baking pan and spray the top of each piece of fish with the olive oil spray.

3. In a small bowl, mix together the Parmesan, almond flour, mustard, Worcestershire sauce, and salt to make a topping for the fish.

4. Top each piece of fish with an equal amount of the Parmesan mixture and pat it down to keep it in place. Spritz the top with olive oil spray so it will crisp up in the oven.

5. Bake for 15 minutes, or until the crust is golden. Serve warm.

TIP: Serve this recipe with Tartar Sauce (page 129).

PER SERVING: FAT 31%; PROTEIN 61%; CARBS 8%; Calories: 253; Total fat: 9g; Protein: 37g; Total carbs: 9g; Fiber: 1g; Net carbs: 8g; Sodium: 801mg; Iron: 1mg

Crab-Stuffed Portobello Mushrooms

PREP TIME: 10 minutes | **COOK TIME:** 15 minutes | **SERVES 2**

I love stuffed mushrooms, and filling them with crab packs in the protein you need for clean keto eating. I used claw crab because it is the most cost-effective fresh crab, but you can use lump crab, too. Avoid imitation crab, however, as it is high in carbs. This dish is best served hot and eaten immediately.

2 portobello mushrooms

2 ounces cream cheese

1 scallion, finely chopped

4 ounces crab claw meat

4 tablespoons grated Cheddar cheese

4 tablespoons grated Parmesan cheese

1 teaspoon Italian Spice Blend (page 126)

½ teaspoon kosher salt

3 tablespoons crushed pork rinds

Olive oil spray, for topping

1. Preheat the oven to 400°F. Line a rimmed baking sheet with parchment paper.

2. Clean the mushrooms with a paper towel by gently rubbing the caps to remove any dirt. Remove the stems and scrape out the grills. Place the mushrooms on the baking sheet, cap-side down.

3. In a medium, microwave-safe bowl, combine the cream cheese and scallion. Microwave for 20 seconds, then stir until combined.

4. Add the crab, Cheddar, Parmesan, Italian spice blend, and salt. Divide the mixture between the mushrooms and fill the mushroom caps. Sprinkle the pork rinds over the tops and spray generously with olive oil spray.

5. Bake for 15 minutes, or until crunchy and golden brown.

TIP: For the topping, you can swap the pork rinds with a mixture of 2 tablespoons almond flour and 2 tablespoons Parmesan.

PER SERVING: FAT 59%; PROTEIN 31%; CARBS 10%; Calories: 274; Total fat: 18g; Protein: 22g; Total carbs: 7g; Fiber: 1g; Net carbs: 6g; Sodium: 842mg; Iron: 1mg

Tilapia Bisque

PREP TIME: 5 minutes | **COOK TIME:** 20 minutes | **SERVES 2**

Bisque is a smooth and creamy soup embellished with chunks of seafood. I have chosen a mild fish so I could showcase the beautiful herbs and spices in this dish. Combining protein and fats with these rich flavors results in a perfect keto meal.

½ pound tilapia fillet

1 teaspoon kosher salt

1 teaspoon garlic powder

½ teaspoon lemon pepper

1 cup chicken broth

1 cup heavy cream

1½ ounces finely chopped
   baby spinach

¼ cup grated
   Parmesan cheese

¼ teaspoon ground
   turmeric

¼ teaspoon cayenne pepper

1. Season the fish on both sides with the salt, garlic powder, and lemon pepper, and set them aside on a plate.

2. In a nonstick frying pan over medium-high heat, combine the chicken broth and cream and bring it to a boil.

3. Reduce the heat to medium, add the spinach, Parmesan, turmeric, and cayenne pepper and whisk until combined. Simmer the sauce, whisking frequently to scrape the bottom of the pan as the Parmesan tends to settle, for 2 or 3 minutes.

4. Add the fish and cook for 5 minutes. Using a small spatula, stir the fish into the sauce. It will break up a little, which is fine.

5. Reduce the heat to low and simmer, stirring once or twice and scraping the bottom of the pan, for 10 minutes.

6. Spoon the bisque into bowls and serve hot.

TIP: Avoid over-stirring so the fish won't shred too much. It's better in chunks.

PER SERVING: FAT 75%; PROTEIN 20%; CARBS 5%; Calories: 585; Total fat: 50g; Protein: 30g; Total carbs: 7g; Fiber: 1g; Net carbs: 6g; Sodium: 928mg; Iron: 1mg

Dill Dip, page 115

Snacks and Sides

Oven-Cooked Bacon

PREP TIME: 5 minutes | **COOK TIME:** 15 minutes | **MAKES 12 BACON PIECES**

When you're looking for protein and saturated fat (and the best-tasting pork product ever), bacon is your meat of choice. There are many different ways to cook it, but the easiest and least messy is in the oven. It comes out crispy and extra delicious. Eat it on its own as a snack, use a few slices as a side dish, or chop it up to make bacon crumbles to top a salad or sprinkle on Mozzarella Bites (page 114).

12 strips bacon

1. Preheat the oven to 400°F. Line a large baking sheet with parchment paper and place an oven-safe rack on top.

2. Place the strips of bacon on the rack in a single layer.

3. Bake for 15 minutes, or until just crisp. If you like your bacon crispier, bake for 5 minutes more.

TIP: With meal prepping in mind, you could double the recipe, chop up any leftover bacon, store it in an airtight container in the refrigerator, and use it as bacon bits over the next few days.

PER SERVING (2 BACON STRIPS): FAT 71%; PROTEIN 28%; CARBS 1%; Calories: 89; Total fat: 7g; Protein: 6g; Total carbs: 0g; Fiber: 0g; Net carbs: 0g; Sodium: 355mg; Iron: 0mg

C1, C2, C3, C4, CK

Perfect Ground Beef

PREP TIME: 5 minutes | **COOK TIME:** 10 minutes | **SERVES 4**

When you want something simple and tasty in a hurry, cooked ground beef is a great choice. It is quick and easy to prepare and full of natural flavor. I would recommend using good-quality ground chuck with a high-fat content, ideally 80 percent lean and 20 percent fat. You'll be amazed at how satisfying it is. If you're in the first few weeks of the reset plan, omit the cayenne, paprika, and red pepper flakes.

1 pound ground chuck beef

1 teaspoon kosher salt

½ teaspoon cayenne pepper (optional)

1 teaspoon paprika (optional)

½ teaspoon red pepper flakes (optional)

1. Let the meat sit at room temperature for 30 minutes before cooking it.

2. Heat a cast-iron pan over medium-high heat for 2 minutes. Add the beef and, using a sturdy spatula, break up the meat and stir it as it cooks, for 4 or 5 minutes.

3. Reduce the heat to medium, add the salt, cayenne pepper (if using), paprika (if using), and pepper flakes (if using), and cook until browned and the internal temperature reaches 160°F, 4 or 5 minutes more.

4. Leftovers can be stored in an airtight container and refrigerated for up to 4 days or frozen for up to 3 months.

PER SERVING: FAT 51%; PROTEIN 49%; CARBS 0%; Calories: 200; Total fat: 11g; Protein: 23g; Total carbs: 0g; Fiber: 0g; Net carbs: 0g; Sodium: 366mg; Iron: 3mg

C3, C4, CK

Salted Butter and Buttermilk

PREP TIME: 15 minutes | **MAKES ½ CUP BUTTER AND ½ CUP BUTTERMILK**

With only two ingredients, you can make two different and very delicious homemade staples: salted butter and buttermilk. I get such a sense of accomplishment when I make my own butter and smother my steaks with it. And it's so easy! The butter keeps for up to 3 weeks in the refrigerator as long as you squeeze out as much buttermilk as you can. The buttermilk can be refrigerated for 2 weeks.

1 cup heavy cream
½ teaspoon kosher salt

TO MAKE THE BUTTERMILK

1. Pour the cream into a deep bowl and using an electric hand mixer or a stand mixer, beat on high speed for 5 minutes. Scrape down the sides of the bowl and continue to beat for 5 minutes more, moving the beaters in a circular motion.

2. The cream will start to resemble pale, scrambled eggs. Continue to beat on high until the mixture separates, about 4 minutes more. You will see liquid pool at the bottom of the bowl; this is buttermilk.

3. Strain the mixture into a colander set over a bowl. Using your hands, squeeze the solids to release any excess buttermilk into the bowl.

4. Store the buttermilk in an airtight container.

TO MAKE THE BUTTER

5. Rinse the remaining solids in the strainer under cold water, and continue squeezing, until the liquid coming out runs clear, about 1 minute. Press the butter into a shallow bowl with your fingers and pour off any remaining liquid.

6. Sprinkle the salt over the butter and, using a fork, mash it together, making sure the salt is equally distributed.

7. Store the butter in a small glass container with a lid.

BUTTERMILK: PER SERVING (2 TABLESPOONS): FAT 48%; PROTEIN 21%; CARBS 31%; Calories: 19; Total Fat: 1g; Protein: 1g, Total Carbs: 1g; Fiber: 0g; Net Carbs: 1g; Sodium: 32mg; Iron: 0mg

BUTTER: PER SERVING (2 TABLESPOONS): FAT 99%; PROTEIN 1%; CARBS 0%; Calories: 204; Total fat: 23g; Protein: 0g; Total carbs: 0g; Fiber: 0g; Net carbs: 0g; Sodium: 183mg; Iron: 0mg

Cheese Shells

PREP TIME: 5 minutes | **COOK TIME:** 10 minutes | **SERVES 2**

This amazing recipe is the ideal vehicle for tacos, and these shells are carb-free. Bonus—they're made with just one ingredient. Crazy, right? I have experimented with various cheeses and found that Cheddar works the best, but feel free to try others. Fill them with shredded chicken, guacamole, and salsa for a tasty and guilt-free meal.

1 cup grated Cheddar cheese, divided

1. Heat a small, nonstick saucepan over medium-low heat for 1 minute. Sprinkle ½ cup of cheese over the bottom of the pan, to form a circle.

2. Cook until the cheese makes uniform bubbles, about 2½ minutes.

3. Remove the pan from the heat and let cool for 3 minutes. Using a spatula, release the edges first, then remove the cheese shell and place it on a plate. Gently fold the shell over, forming a taco shape. Let cool completely.

4. Repeat with the remaining ½ cup of cheese to make the second cheese shell. Blot any excess oil from the shells with a paper towel. Serve with your favorite fillings.

TIP: I always buy large blocks of cheese and grate them myself. Pre-grated cheese includes a caking ingredient that stops it from sticking together and adds unwanted carbs. You can buy electric cheese graters that can shred an entire block of cheese in 1 minute.

PER SERVING: FAT 75%; PROTEIN 24%; CARBS 1%; Calories: 229; Total fat: 19g; Protein: 14g; Total carbs: 1g; Fiber: 0g; Net carbs: 1g; Sodium: 364mg; Iron: 0mg

C3, C4, CK

Queso

PREP TIME: 5 minutes | **COOK TIME:** 10 minutes | **MAKES 2 CUPS**

Queso is such a treat, and it's fun to serve when you entertain. If you eat carnivore, simply use it as a decadent sauce for your main meal. Pour it over the Garlic and Herb Pork Loin Chop (page 69) or drizzle it over a Turkey Burger (page 85). For a clean keto option, use it as a dip for carrot and celery sticks. It's best to eat queso the same day you make it, and it's so tasty you won't have any trouble doing that.

1 cup heavy cream

2 ounces cream cheese

1 cup grated
  Cheddar cheese

¼ teaspoon kosher salt

Pinch freshly ground
  black pepper

½ teaspoon freshly
  squeezed lime juice

1. In a small saucepan, bring the cream to a simmer over medium-low heat, about 2 minutes.

2. Add the cream cheese and, using a whisk, gently mix it into the cream. Add the Cheddar, salt, pepper, and lime juice and cook, stirring constantly, until the mixture is fully melted and combined.

3. Reduce the heat to low and continue to cook until the mixture is thickened, 2 or 3 minutes more.

TIP: I like Cheddar for this recipe, but you can use a different cheese if you prefer. It just needs to be a cheese that is meltable. My husband loves to use Buffalo Cheddar to add some spice.

PER SERVING (¼ CUP): FAT 87%; PROTEIN 10%; CARBS 3%; Calories: 184; Total fat: 18g; Protein: 4g; Total carbs: 1g; Fiber: 0g; Net carbs: 1g; Sodium: 167mg; Iron: 0mg

Mozzarella Bites

PREP TIME: 5 minutes | **COOK TIME:** 10 minutes | **SERVES 2**

Mozzarella bites make a tasty little snack, and sometimes I serve them as a side dish with recipes like Garlic Shrimp (page 97). If you're not a fan of jalapeño peppers, you can omit them or add some bacon crumbles on top instead. I would recommend eating these right away because they are at their best when they are warm from the oven.

Avocado oil spray, for greasing

1 cup shredded mozzarella cheese

1 tablespoon finely chopped jalapeño pepper

1. Preheat the oven to 400°F. Spray a little avocado oil into a six-cup silicone muffin pan.

2. Divide the mozzarella equally among the six cups, about 2 tablespoons per cup. Sprinkle the jalapeño pepper equally over each bite.

3. Bake for 8 minutes. Let cool in the pan for 5 minutes. Carefully ease the mozzarella bites out of the tray and serve immediately.

TIP: Grate your own mozzarella rather than buying pre-shredded cheese, which has added ingredients that will increase your carb intake. Shredding your own is cheaper, too.

PER SERVING (3 BITES): FAT 65%; PROTEIN 32%; CARBS 3%; Calories: 168; Total fat: 12g; Protein: 12g; Total carbs: 1g; Fiber: 0g; Net carbs: 1g; Sodium: 351mg; Iron: 0mg

CK

Dill Dip

PREP TIME: 5 minutes | **MAKES ABOUT ⅔ CUP**

Fresh dill has the leading role in this delicious dip and everything comes together in just 5 minutes. Enjoy it as an accompaniment in recipes like Delicious Sirloin (page 54) or dip your favorite crudités or even pork rinds in its creamy goodness.

⅓ cup sour cream

¼ cup avocado oil mayonnaise

1 tablespoon dried minced onion

¼ teaspoon kosher salt

2 tablespoons finely chopped fresh dill

½ tablespoon finely chopped fresh parsley

1. In a small bowl, whisk together the sour cream and mayonnaise.

2. Add the onion, salt, dill, and parsley, and whisk until thoroughly combined.

3. Serve with your favorite dippers. Store any leftovers in an airtight container and refrigerate for up to 1 week.

TIP: To take this dip to the next level, mix in some bacon crumbles.

PER SERVING (APPROX. 2 TABLESPOONS): FAT 77%; PROTEIN 4%; CARBS 19%; Calories: 59; Total fat: 5g; Protein: 1g; Total carbs: 3g; Fiber: 0g; Net carbs: 3g; Sodium: 84mg; Iron: 1mg

Lemon and Garlic Asparagus

PREP TIME: 5 minutes | **COOK TIME:** 15 minutes | **SERVES 2**

Roasting asparagus makes it a little crispy on the outside and tender on the inside and gives it a lovely caramelized taste. It pairs nicely with nearly any kind of meat.

2 tablespoons grated Parmesan cheese

1 tablespoon chopped fresh parsley

2 teaspoons dried minced garlic

½ teaspoon kosher salt

¼ teaspoon freshly ground black pepper

½ pound asparagus, trimmed

2 tablespoons olive oil

Juice of ½ small lemon

1. Preheat the oven to 400°F. Line a rimmed baking sheet with parchment paper.

2. In a small bowl, mix together the Parmesan, parsley, dried garlic, salt, and pepper.

3. Arrange the asparagus in one layer on the prepared baking sheet and drizzle it with the olive oil. Sprinkle the Parmesan mixture evenly over the top. Squeeze the lemon juice over everything.

4. Bake for 10 to 15 minutes, until the asparagus is a little crispy on the outside and tender in the middle.

TIP: For an added kick of flavor, add 1 teaspoon of red pepper flakes to the Parmesan mixture.

PER SERVING: FAT 78%; PROTEIN 8%; CARBS 14%; Calories: 171; Total fat: 15g; Protein: 4g; Total carbs: 7g; Fiber: 3g; Net carbs: 4g; Sodium: 385mg; Iron: 3mg

CK

Cauliflower Rice

PREP TIME: 5 minutes | **COOK TIME:** 10 minutes | **SERVES 2**

As you probably already know, cauliflower rice is one of the most essential sides when eating keto. This recipe is so flavorful, it will satisfy any of your fried-rice cravings. It is a versatile dish that can be used as an accompaniment or base to any protein dish.

1 tablespoon salted butter

½ small carrot,
    finely chopped

2 tablespoons chicken broth

1 scallion, finely chopped

1 celery stalk,
    finely chopped

1 tablespoon soy sauce

1 garlic clove, minced

½ teaspoon white
    wine vinegar

½ teaspoon garlic powder

½ teaspoon kosher salt

½ teaspoon freshly ground
    black pepper

½ teaspoon lemongrass
    paste (optional)

2 cups cauliflower rice

1 egg, whisked

1. In a medium, nonstick frying pan, melt the butter over medium heat. Reduce the heat to low, add the carrots and chicken broth, and let cook, covered, for 2 or 3 minutes.

2. Increase the heat to medium, add the scallion, celery, soy sauce, garlic clove, vinegar, garlic powder, salt, pepper, lemongrass paste (if using), and cauliflower, and sauté for 5 minutes.

3. Make a well in the center of the mixture and add the egg. Cook for 1 minute. Stir the egg into the rice mixture and cook until set. Serve warm.

TIP: You can vary this dish by swapping in other vegetables, such as chopped bell peppers or thinly sliced leeks.

PER SERVING: FAT 57%; PROTEIN 17%; CARBS 26%; Calories: 133; Total fat: 9g; Protein: 7g; Total carbs: 9g; Fiber: 3g; Net carbs: 6g; Sodium: 686mg; Iron: 1mg

CK

Lyonnaise Faux-tatoes

PREP TIME: 20 minutes | **COOK TIME:** 30 minutes | **SERVES 4**

Inspired by the French dish from Lyon, this recipe supplies the same buttery flavors without the carbs. Cooked radishes and rutabaga acquire an earthy, slightly sweet flavor that will make you believe you are eating potatoes! I particularly like this dish alongside Blackened Cod (page 94).

2 pounds rutabaga, peeled and thinly sliced

3 ounces radishes, peeled and thinly sliced

2 cups water

2 tablespoons olive oil

1 medium onion, thinly sliced

3 garlic cloves, minced

½ cup (1 stick) salted butter

Kosher salt, for seasoning

Freshly ground black pepper, for seasoning

1. Place the rutabagas, radishes, and water in a large, microwave-safe bowl and microwave for 14 minutes. Drain and set the vegetables aside.

2. While the vegetables are cooking, in a medium, cast-iron pan, heat the olive oil over high heat for 1 minute.

3. Add the onion to the skillet and sauté for 8 minutes. Turn off the heat. Mix the garlic into the onions.

4. Preheat the oven to 425°F.

5. Transfer the onions to a bowl and set aside. Melt the butter in the skillet over low heat.

6. Arrange half of the rutabaga slices in a single layer in the skillet. Spread half the onions over the rutabaga and season with salt and pepper. Spread the radishes on top of the onions.

7. Spread the remaining half of the onions over the radishes and then make a top layer using the remaining half of the rutabaga. Season with salt.

8. Put the skillet in the oven and bake for 30 minutes, or until the faux-tatoes crisp on top. Serve warm.

PER SERVING: FAT 73%; PROTEIN 3%; CARBS 24%; Calories: 365; Total fat: 30g; Protein: 3g; Total carbs: 24g; Fiber: 6g; Net carbs: 18g; Sodium: 258mg; Iron: 1mg

CK

Peanut Butter Cookies

PREP TIME: 10 minutes | **COOK TIME:** 10 minutes, plus about 30 minutes to cool | **MAKES 10 COOKIES**

Peanut butter cookies are loved by children and adults alike, and in this version I added orange zest to give them a delightfully unexpected flavor twist. Relax on the sofa with a guilt-free cookie, a cup of tea, and start bingeing on your favorite streaming series. The cookies will stay fresh stored in an airtight container and can be refrigerated for up to 1 week or frozen for up to 3 months.

1 cup unsweetened
   peanut butter
1 egg, at room temperature
¼ cup allulose
1 tablespoon brown sugar
   erythritol
1 tablespoon freshly
   squeezed orange juice
1 tablespoon orange zest
⅓ cup coconut flour
¼ cup slivered almonds
1 teaspoon almond extract
½ teaspoon baking powder
¼ teaspoon xanthan gum
Pinch kosher salt

1. Preheat the oven to 350°F. Line a baking sheet with parchment paper or a silicone mat.

2. In a large bowl, combine the peanut butter, egg, allulose, erythritol, orange juice, and orange zest. Using an electric hand mixer, beat until smooth.

3. Add the coconut flour, slivered almonds, almond extract, baking powder, xanthan gum, and salt, and beat until the mixture is completely combined. The mixture should be stiff like cookie dough.

4. Using a medium ice cream scoop or a large serving spoon, portion out 10 cookies onto the prepared baking sheet. Flatten each cookie using the base of a drinking glass until they are ½-inch thick.

5. Bake for 10 minutes, until golden brown.

6. Let sit until completely cool, about 30 minutes. Try not to eat them all at once.

TIP: Allulose is a great choice for a sweetener, as it has little or no effect on blood glucose or insulin levels.

PER SERVING (1 COOKIE): FAT 75%; PROTEIN 16%; CARBS 9%; Calories: 180; Total fat: 15g; Protein: 7g; Total carbs: 11g; Fiber: 2g; Net carbs: 9g; Sodium: 27mg; Iron: 1mg

Peanut Butter Cream

PREP TIME: 5 minutes | **SERVES 4**

Peanut butter is such a treat, but when you are counting carbs and calories, it can really add up. Here is a little trick I came up with to reduce those carbs and still get all the peanut butter flavor you want.

¼ cup heavy cream

¼ cup unsweetened peanut butter

⅛ teaspoon almond extract

1. Pour the cream into a small bowl. Using an electric hand mixer with the whisk attachment, beat the cream until it begins to thicken, about 2 minutes.

2. Add the peanut butter and almond extract and continue to beat for about 1 minute more.

3. Store any leftovers in an airtight container in the refrigerator for up to 3 days.

TIP: If your sweet tooth is working overtime, you can add 1 tablespoon of your favorite, powdered keto-friendly sweetener; just remember to add it to your macros.

PER SERVING (2 TABLESPOONS): FAT 89%; PROTEIN 10%; CARBS 1%; Calories: 140; Total fat: 14g; Protein: 4g; Total carbs: 2g; Fiber: 1g; Net carbs: 1g; Sodium: 8mg; Iron: mg

From left to right: Italian Spice Blend, page 126; Smoky Spice Blend, page 124

CHAPTER 8

Staples

Smoky Spice Blend

PREP TIME: 5 minutes | **MAKES ¼ CUP**

This blend has a big personality. Its intense flavor comes from smoked paprika (a favorite of mine) and a spicy dose of cayenne pepper. It gives any fish, meat, or chicken dish a lovely kick, and you can use it as a rub or a seasoning. I love this blend on Smoky Turkey Cutlets (page 88).

3 teaspoons smoked paprika

2 teaspoons mustard powder

1½ teaspoons garlic powder

1½ teaspoons onion powder

1½ teaspoons kosher salt

1 teaspoon cayenne pepper

1 teaspoon ground cumin

½ teaspoon freshly ground black pepper

1. In a small bowl, mix together the paprika, mustard powder, garlic powder, onion powder, salt, cayenne pepper, cumin, and black pepper.

2. Transfer the mixture to a small, airtight container and store at room temperature for up to 6 months. Shake the container well before using.

TIP: You can also store this in a jar with an airtight lid. Write the name of the spice blend on a label and affix it to the jar to avoid confusion if you make a few different spice blends.

PER SERVING (2 TEASPOONS): FAT 15%; PROTEIN 32%; CARBS 53%; Calories: 14; Total fat: 1g; Protein: 1g; Total carbs: 2g; Fiber: 1g; Net carbs: 1g; Sodium: 293mg; Iron: 1mg

C4, CK

Seafood Spice Blend

PREP TIME: 5 minutes | **MAKES ¼ CUP**

To me, dill is one of the most delicious herbs and possibly the most underused. It is the hero of this blend, which adds a bright, botanical flavor to any fish dish. I recommend using lemon pepper as opposed to black pepper, as it pairs so well with all varieties of fish. Try this blend with Salmon Fritters (page 99).

3 teaspoons dried dill

3 teaspoons onion powder

3 teaspoons dried parsley

2 teaspoons garlic powder

1 teaspoon lemon pepper

1. In a small bowl, mix together the dill, onion powder, parsley, garlic powder, and lemon pepper.

2. Transfer the mixture to an airtight container and store at room temperature for up to 6 months. Shake the container well before using.

PER SERVING (2 TEASPOONS): FAT 5%; PROTEIN 12%; CARBS 83%; Calories: 10; Total fat: 0g; Protein: 0g; Total carbs: 2g; Fiber: 1g; Net carbs: 1g; Sodium: 3mg; Iron: 0mg

Italian Spice Blend

PREP TIME: 5 minutes | **MAKES ¼ CUP**

This is a mild-flavored seasoning with a carefully balanced mix of herbs that's suitable to add to almost any savory dish. This has become a go-to mix for me and I use it all the time. I like the convenience of having it made up ahead of time. Enjoy it with Crab-Stuffed Portobello Mushrooms (page 104).

3 teaspoons dried rosemary

3 teaspoons dried basil

3 teaspoons dried thyme

2 teaspoons garlic powder

1 teaspoon dried oregano

1. In a small bowl, mix together the rosemary, basil, thyme, garlic powder, and oregano.

2. Transfer the mixture to an airtight container and store it at room temperature for up to 6 months. Shake the container well before using.

PER SERVING (2 TEASPOONS): FAT 16%; PROTEIN 11%; CARBS 73%; Calories: 8; Total fat: 0g; Protein: 0g; Total carbs: 2g; Fiber: 1g; Net carbs: 1g; Sodium: 2mg; Iron: 1mg

C4, CK

Everything Bagel Spice Blend

PREP TIME: 5 minutes | **MAKES ¼ CUP**

This blend is inspired by the now-famous everything bagel craze and it enhances the flavors of more than just bagels. You can add it to almost any savory dish. Sprinkle it over any egg dish to give the finished recipe an extra boost. I use it all the time in Baked Eggs (page 42) and Poached Eggs (page 40). The combined colors of the ingredients look great sprinkled over the food, too.

4 teaspoons poppy seeds

4 teaspoons sesame seeds

1½ teaspoons dried minced garlic

1½ teaspoons dried minced onion

1 teaspoon kosher salt

1. In a small bowl, mix together the poppy seeds, sesame seeds, dried garlic, dried onion, and salt.

2. Transfer the mixture to an airtight container and store it at room temperature for up to 6 months. Shake the container well before using.

TIP: Adjust the quantity of the ingredients to suit your taste; for example, if you are a garlic lover, add more.

PER SERVING (2 TEASPOONS): FAT 64%; PROTEIN 12%; CARBS 24%; Calories: 25; Total fat: 2g; Protein: 1g; Total carbs: 2g; Fiber: 1g; Net carbs: 1g; Sodium: 196mg; Iron: 0mg

C4, CK

Chicken Bone Broth

PREP TIME: 5 minutes | **COOK TIME:** 4 hours | **MAKES ABOUT 8 CUPS**

Homemade chicken bone broth is packed full of vitamins and minerals, including iron, calcium, and magnesium. It can help aid digestion, reduce inflammation, and offer joint protection. Full of collagen, it provides the body with the amino acids used for both muscular and cell renewal. Bone broth is a helpful addition to a carnivore diet because it is so flavorful and full of bioavailable nutrition.

Carcass, neck, and giblets
  of 1 whole chicken

2 to 3 pounds chicken wings

2 small onions, halved

2 celery stalks

2 carrots, trimmed

10 peppercorns

2 teaspoons kosher salt

2 sprigs rosemary

2 sprigs thyme

2 bay leaves

2½ quarts water

1. In a large Dutch oven, combine the chicken carcass, neck, giblets, chicken wings, onions, celery, carrots, peppercorns, salt, rosemary, thyme, bay leaves, and water and bring to a boil over high heat. Continue to boil for 3 or 4 minutes.

2. Reduce the heat to medium to simmer. Partially cover the pan to allow the steam to escape and let cook for 4 hours.

3. Using a slotted spoon, remove the solid ingredients and discard them. Pour the broth into a fine-mesh sieve set over a large saucepan. Bring the broth to a boil over high heat and, using a large spoon, skim any fat off the top.

4. Let the broth cool for a few minutes. Taste and add more salt if desired.

TIP: I store my broth in mason jars in the fridge for up to 1 week but it can also be frozen for up to 3 months. If you are freezing it to use as a base in other recipes, freeze it in ice cube trays. You can use a couple of cubes at a time, depending on what you need.

PER SERVING (½ CUP): FAT 20%; PROTEIN 80%; CARBS 0%; Calories: 45; Total fat: 1g; Protein: 8g; Total carbs: 0g; Fiber: 0g; Net carbs: 0g; Sodium: 167mg; Iron: 1mg

C4, CK

Tartar Sauce

PREPARATION: 10 minutes | **MAKES ABOUT ¾ CUP**

Tartar sauce is a classic accompaniment for any fish dish. The combination of the dill and the acidity of the lemon balances out any strong fishy flavors. It takes me straight back to my UK childhood and my beloved fish and chips. I love serving this alongside Blackened Cod (page 94).

½ cup avocado oil mayonnaise

1 tablespoon freshly squeezed lemon juice

1 dill pickle spear, finely chopped

½ tablespoon dried dill

1 teaspoon Worcestershire sauce

½ teaspoon kosher salt

½ teaspoon freshly ground black pepper

1. In a small bowl, mix together the mayonnaise and lemon juice.

2. Add the dill pickle, dill, Worcestershire sauce, salt, and pepper and stir until combined.

3. Transfer to an airtight container and store in the refrigerator for up to 1 week.

TIP: Feel free to add more dill pickle for extra crunch.

PER SERVING (2 TABLESPOONS) FAT 96%; PROTEIN 1%; CARBS 3%; Calories: 73; Total fat: 8g; Protein: 0g; Total carbs: 1g; Fiber: 0g; Net carbs: 1g; Sodium: 271mg; Iron: 0mg

Loaded Sour Cream

PREP TIME: 10 minutes | **MAKES ABOUT 1 CUP**

Sour cream is simply cultured cream, so it has practically zero carbs, which makes it an excellent accompaniment to most keto and carnivore dishes. In this recipe, I've embellished sour cream with scallion and cheddar to create a lovely dip that can also be used to accompany any protein dish. Try it with the Delicious Sirloin (page 54) and the Strip Steak (page 55).

½ cup sour cream

1 scallion, finely chopped

½ cup grated
   Cheddar cheese

1 tablespoon chopped mild
   banana pepper

Kosher salt, for seasoning

Freshly ground black
   pepper, for seasoning

1. In a small bowl, mix together the sour cream, scallion, Cheddar, banana pepper, and salt and pepper to taste.

2. Transfer to an airtight container and store in the refrigerator for up to 1 week.

TIP: Try adding your favorite chopped vegetables to this recipe, or add some crumbled bacon for extra protein.

PER SERVING (2 TABLESPOONS): FAT 81%; PROTEIN 14%; CARBS 5%; Calories: 57; Total fat: 5g; Protein: 2g; Total carbs: 1g; Fiber: 0g; Net carbs: 1g; Sodium: 72mg; Iron: 0mg

CK

Tomato Salsa

PREP TIME: 15 minutes | **SERVES 4**

Fresh produce and lively flavors come together in this delicious chunky salsa. I prefer to chop the ingredients by hand, to control the size of the tomatoes. Though you can enjoy it right after you make it, this salsa is even better if you let it marinate and develop additional flavor overnight.

10 cherry tomatoes, finely chopped

½ cup canned diced tomatoes, with juices

1 scallion, finely chopped

¼ cup finely chopped red onion

Zest and juice of ½ lime

1 tablespoon chopped fresh cilantro or parsley

¼ teaspoon paprika

⅛ teaspoon ground ginger

⅛ teaspoon cayenne pepper

2 garlic cloves, minced

Kosher salt, for seasoning

Freshly ground black pepper, for seasoning

1. In a medium bowl, combine the cherry tomatoes and diced tomatoes with their juices.

2. Add the scallion, red onion, lime zest and juice, cilantro, paprika, ginger, cayenne, garlic, salt, and pepper to taste. Mix well.

3. Serve immediately or transfer the salsa to an airtight container and refrigerate for up to 5 days.

TIP: For a little heat, add 1 tablespoon of chopped jalapeño pepper.

PER SERVING: FAT 8%; PROTEIN 11%; CARBS 81%; Calories: 22; Total fat: 0g; Protein: 1g; Total carbs: 5g; Fiber: 1g; Net carbs: 4g; Sodium: 5mg; Iron: 0mg

MEASUREMENT CONVERSIONS

Volume Equivalents (Liquid)

US STANDARD	US STANDARD (OUNCES)	METRIC (APPROXIMATE)
2 tablespoons	1 fl. oz.	30 mL
¼ cup	2 fl. oz.	60 mL
½ cup	4 fl. oz.	120 mL
1 cup	8 fl. oz.	240 mL
1½ cups	12 fl. oz.	355 mL
2 cups or 1 pint	16 fl. oz.	475 mL
4 cups or 1 quart	32 fl. oz.	1 L
1 gallon or 4 quarts	128 fl. oz.	4 L

Oven Temperatures

FAHRENHEIT	CELSIUS (APPROXIMATE)
250°F	120°C
300°F	150°C
325°F	165°C
350°F	180°C
375°F	190°C
400°F	200°C
425°F	220°C
450°F	230°C

Volume Equivalents (Dry)

US STANDARD	METRIC (APPROXIMATE)
⅛ teaspoon	0.5 mL
¼ teaspoon	1 mL
½ teaspoon	2 mL
¾ teaspoon	4 mL
1 teaspoon	5 mL
1 tablespoon	15 mL
¼ cup	59 mL
⅓ cup	79 mL
½ cup	118 mL
⅔ cup	156 mL
¾ cup	177 mL
1 cup	235 mL
2 cups or 1 pint	475 mL
3 cups	700 mL
4 cups or 1 quart	1 L

Weight Equivalents

US STANDARD	METRIC (APPROXIMATE)
½ ounce	15 g
1 ounce	30 g
2 ounces	60 g
4 ounces	115 g
8 ounces	225 g
12 ounces	340 g
16 ounces or 1 pound	455 g

RESOURCES

BOOKS

Baker, Shawn. *The Carnivore Diet*. Las Vegas: Victory Belt, 2019.

Silverstein, Michael. *New Keto Cooking: Fresh Ideas for Delicious Low-Carb Meals at Home*. Salem, MA: Page Street Publishing, 2020.

Taubes, Gary. *The Case for Keto: Rethinking Weight Control and the Science and Practice of Low-Carb/High-Fat Eating*. New York: Anchor, 2020.

Teicholz, Nina. *The Big Fat Surprise: Why Butter, Meat, and Cheese Belong in a Healthy Diet*. New York: Simon & Schuster, 2014.

DOCUMENTARIES

Hyman, Mark, Nina Teicholz, and Gary Taubes. *Fat Fiction*, 2020.

Tortorich, Vinnie. *Fat: A Documentary*, 2019.

PODCASTS

Diet Doctor Podcast with Dr. Bret Scher

Fast Keto with Ketogenic Girl with Vanessa Spina

INSTAGRAM

Mel Brown @ladymelskitchen

Maria Emmerich @mariaemmerich

Rubio Fuerte @rubiofuerte

Dr. Ryan Lowery @ketogeniccom @ryanplowery

Shawn Wells @shawnwells

REFERENCES

Epilepsy Foundation. *Ketogenic Diet.* Epilepsy.com/learn /treating-seizures-and-epilepsy/dietary-therapies/ketogenic-diet.

Kendrick, Malcolm. *The Great Cholesterol Con: The Truth about What Really Causes Heart Disease and How to Avoid It.* London: John Blake Publishing, 2007.

Pobiner, Briana. "Evidence for Meat-Eating by Early Humans." *Nature Education Knowledge* 4, no. 6 (2013): 1.

INDEX

Acknowledgments

Thank you to my husband and children for their support and patience during the writing of this book. Dan, you stepped up, and now you know what mom life looks like. You allowed me the creative space I needed to get this book written. For that I'm so grateful. To Lottie, Ben, Raffi, and Luca, thank you for being the most honest food critics. To my eldest, Natasha, her husband, Ben, and their new baby, Aurelia, your belief in me is what gives me the confidence to reach for the stars. You have supported me on this incredible journey that preoccupied my every waking thought for many months. To my keto friends: To have constant support from a community of people that all share the same love of food lifts my spirit every day. Lastly, thanks to my mum, who taught me the joy of cooking.

About the Author

 **Mel Brown** is a self-taught British chef, recipe creator, and food photographer. She lives in the United States with her husband and children. She began her research on health and nutrition five years ago. On her popular Instagram page (@ladymel-skitchen) and website (Ketokweenla.com), she shares her knowledge about the keto carnivore diet and her love of cooking with thousands of loyal followers. She has previously written two keto cookbooks. Mel strongly believes in the importance of positive language around food, and she has taught her children the same love of food that she has. She continually shares her knowledge on health and nutrition with her family, and they all enjoy low-carb eating together.

CPSIA information can be obtained
at www.ICGtesting.com
Printed in the USA
LVHW021107251021
701390LV00002B/3

9 781648 764097